LOVE YOU

SPECIAL EDITION

THE LATINA EDITION

SPECIAL EDITION

LOVE
YOU

The

Latina

Edition

Dinorah Nieves, PhD

ELEVATION PRESS

New York 2018

Elevation Press
Yonkers, NY 10710

Love YOU: The Latina Edition
Copyright © 2018 by Dinorah Nieves, PhD

The author of this book does not dispense medical, psychological or psychiatric advice, nor prescribe the use of any technique as a form of treatment for physical or psychological problems without the advice of a physician or mental health specialist, either directly or indirectly. The intent of the author is only to offer information of a general nature to those looking to explore ways to feel better about themselves and their lives. In the event that you use any of the information in this book for yourself or another, the author and the publisher assume no responsibility for your actions or feelings.

The names of some individuals in this book have been changed.

Cover by Deliz Berrios

Author Photo by Suzanne Bonanno

Manufactured in the United States of America

ISBN-10: 0-9982791-2-9
ISBN-13: 978-0-9982791-2-1

This book is dedicated to my family and friends…
Only standing atop the foundation of love, support and faith
that you built for me, was I able to muster the strength to
finally fall in love with myself… and life!
… A special "thank you" to my mother and father whose
undying and unconditional love have blessed every day of this
incarnation with joy and courage.
… And a humble and love-filled "shout out" to the gorgeous,
inspired and kind man with whom I now share my life; whose
encouragement, patience and vision helped give life to this
book and whose spirit is truly a gift.

… Thank you too, to Lisa Skelton, for your editing eye and
beautiful spirit. May the peace of your soul be forever
remembered.

Contents

Poetic Reflection: Welcome to My World

What you're about to read
Is the documentation of the depressing, exciting, inspiring,
light-guiding journey, that transformed me
Out of my darkest of nights and into my lightest of dreams
It's the reason why I can finally freaking breathe!
It's the way that I learned to finally be me, it's what got me off
my ass and set me free

Sure, I was a wanted, blessed and welcomed baby
Who blossomed into a loved and loving teen
But in the depths of my heart remained this vacancy
And between wanting it filled and just needing to feel seen
I picked boys, then men, who broke my heart in ways hard to
mend, and somehow I just always ended up feeling more and
more lonely
And then loneliness became my king and I his queen
And together we ruled throughout the better part of my
twenties, until pain and sorrow began to come between
And we finally had to face the possibility
That maybe we just weren't meant to be

And I had to finally face the possibility that maybe the damn
problem was me
Maybe it was the ways I thought of love as codependency
Or that nagging or the needing or the wanting and forgiving
Or the independent crap I was trying to pretend I was living
Or the stupid fairy tales and urban fantasies
Maybe the only person who truly needed to learn how to love
me… was me

So, I worked…

I worked on my mind, I worked on my spirit, I worked on my body
I moved seamlessly through each dimension of my wellness, until the cold sweats led to full nights of sleep
I read, and I drew, and I got to know the secrets I had put away in the parts of my mind that were hidden so deep
I dated, and I prayed, and I prayed on many of my dates and I deleted any relationships that didn't make my spirit feel clean
I meditated and learned how to set boundaries
I traveled and exercised and reclaimed my dreams
I worked until my loneliness gave way to wellness and I cried, and I laughed
and contemplated life and death in the cooling waters of my bubble baths
until I finally began to find peace
And then suddenly, as I began to enjoy the sweetest of treats that were laid out as course three, in this buffet of "crae" from which my soul had chosen to eat, I had the most delicious of epiphanies: "Maybe this shit aint just about me!"

I had a story to tell
To the many people who visit the same kind of hell
In search of what they believe will finally be "the one" with whom they're divinely meant to gel
And then find that they have lost themselves
And it hurts so bad that they just want to yell
"HELP ME, PLEASE."

That's why I wrote the pages that you're about to read
Cause there's a time when you just simply have to ask yourself... is it me?...
What do I need to do to become the greatest version of who I'm meant to be?
What am I teaching others about my worth and my needs?

I mean, what is it about myself that I even truly believe?
Why am I running around trying to convince others to love
me more and better than I seem to love myself?
What if I'm really the one that needs help?"
What if?

That's when you know that it's time to set that love lens to
"selfie"
No filter, no edits, just the raw you that you see
Trust me, there is a big difference between being self-centered
and learning to center yourself, and
the latter is a movement that I want to feed
So, within its mixture of research, memoir, advice and poetry
You'll likely find that this book holds the key
To helping you change what you do, by examining what you
feel and working through what your thoughts might be
And learning to take the steps necessary to begin rewriting
your destiny
Embark with me on this faith-filled, fun-filled, fabulous
journey and let's see where it leads
Your happiness is waiting! Are you ready to proceed?

**... and for my Latinas, reading this and thinking,
perhaps this book isn't for me,
Because self-care is selfish and Latinidad is largely about
focusing on family and the good of the community,
I understand, relate and know how conflicting it can be,
to feel so connected to a collective and still yearn to feel
free, to try to find yourself amid tradition and modernity.
But just as it happened for me, it can happen for you,
because you can love your culture and yourself too,
and there is a way to make change and still stay true...
Keep reading "mamita". Let me show you what to do!**

A Letter to My Latinas

Dear bold, brilliant and brown beauties:

I LOVE being Latina: the history, the languages, the music, the food, the values, the climates, the mixture of influences, traditions and rituals. So, in 2011, I wrote my first book - Latina Biculturalism: An Exploratory Study of Culture, Family, and Self in the Lives of New York-Based Latinas. It was my doctoral dissertation, for which I analyzed survey data and conducted in-depth interviews with 30 educated, urban, adult Latinas. After years of reviewing the field's existing literature on us, I wanted to better understand how our sense of self and our sense of identity was impacted by our Latino culture and by what it tells us is important. It was during that study, that I learned more about marianismo.

As you probably know, "marianismo" is named for the Virgin Mary. It is a cultural framework that defines a "good woman" as one who is "pure," nurturing and saintly. It was introduced by the Spanish who came to conquer and convert the regions that we now think of as Latino America; and it has remained a strong principle by which young Latinas are raised and socialized into womanhood. It's subtly woven into family suggestions and social expectations and communicated faintly, yet forcefully, in what we are encouraged to say, do, wear, believe, etc. as Latinas, and in what ways of life we are discouraged from pursuing. According to marianismo, "a woman is defined by her self-abnegation and by placing family and community above her own needs" (Confresi 1999).

So basically, Latinas are expected to be selfless, self-sacrificing and over-focused on others. My interviews confirmed just that – that while the Latina experience is diverse and changing, many of us are still raised to embody some degree of marianismo. In fact, for as modern as I consider myself, I cannot deny its influence in my own life. As Latinas, most of us are simply not encouraged to or taught how to, prioritize self-care. We learn early on to put the needs of the whole above the wants of the individual and while that serves us in many ways to create beautiful communities, it can be a dangerous saboteur of our individual wellness. Yes, we are stronger together... but only if we each know how strong we are apart. Yes, we are grateful for the gift of fellowship, but we cannot be beholden to it. Yes, we are rich with love, attention and wisdom that was poured into us by large families and communities. And one of the best ways to honor that, is to grow that investment to its greatest potential.

That is why I am releasing this Latina edition. Because we can certainly learn from the Iyanla Vanzants of the world (Thank you Dr. Vanzant for reminding me of the need for this Latina edition). But we need more Latinas, giving other Latinas, permission to be free. And beyond the permission, a playbook set on our field, that highlights our hearts and speaks to our experiences. It's time for a movement within the Latina sisterhood; one where we learn to love ourselves first and to do so, unapologetically. We have enough love to go around. Loving ourselves first does not mean that we stop being a grateful and loving part of our relationships. It means that we come to them full on the inside. Trust me, you can honor both who you are and where you come from. You don't have to sacrifice one for the other. You have the power, the strength... THE RIGHT... to love YOU... first and foremost! #Ámateatimisma

I wrote Love YOU, to help you learn to do just that. In this Latina Edition, I have also added to each part, a section entitled, "Latina Lens," that speaks to some of the emerging themes through the culturally nuanced experiences of us Latinas.

Now, just to be clear, I get that neither the issues I address here, nor the suggestions that I offer, are Latina-specific or true for all Latinas. I know that the reach of marianismo lessens as we modernize. I also know that Latino culture is not the only one that battles with these gender stereotypes, or any stereotypes for that matter. And I am clear that what experiences we share, still vary to differing degrees across the many different ethnic, regional, generational and class groups that make up the diverse category, we call "Latino." As

Latinas, in particular, we are as diverse as we are numerous. Our shades, shapes, educations, experiences and ways of looking at the world are many and span the spectrum. Still, despite our differences, you'll likely find that marianismo is not the only cultural commonality that we share. For instance, most Latinas know what it's like to grow up watching "novelas," with a diet centered around pork, listening to loud music that mixes African drums with Spanish guitars, feeling compelled to live a life that somehow validates our immigrant/migrant parents' sacrifices. Most of us have been warned "que la soledad mata" (loneliness kills), that we shouldn't go out "con la cabeza mojada" (with a wet head) and that we don't want to end up "jamona" (spinster). Many of us have had major injuries and illnesses tended to with Vicks and Bengay and can't get off the phone without saying "Bendición" (blessing) a million times. We enjoy a sandwich from the neighborhood "bodega" as much as we do a Michelin-rated meal, and almost all of us have experienced the guilt of wanting to be independent and free but not wanting to "abandon" our families. Now, I'm a second- generation Puerto Rican from New York, in my 30s, with a huge family. So, this story is mine and the details may vary slightly for you, but the themes I imagine are similar and the emotional experience even more so.

The "Latina Lens" taps into our shared language, customs, beliefs and power as filter for discussing that part's stories, lessons and insights. It's my way of adding to this delicious dish, just the right hint of Adobo (wink). Buen Provecho - I pray you enjoy it!

Introduction

The feeling was at once alarming and numbing. It typically happened around 2 am on nights when I cried myself to sleep, like this one. Anxiety reverberated throughout my body, and my mind filled with the echoes of my countless fears about being alone. "Was I not good enough to be loved? Would I ever find someone to share my life? Was I too independent to be part of a relationship? What was wrong with me? What was wrong with this world? How would I survive so much loneliness? What was the purpose of all this emptiness?" The questions raged on and on, as did the anxiety attacks. The heaving in my chest seemed to go on for hours and all I could focus on was the loneliness I had been left with and the weight of the hollowness I felt whenever I was alone; an emptiness that slid itself like a serpent around my spirit, trapping me in its hold, rendering me helpless and devoid of all strength. What an intense experience to be such a common occurrence; and yet it was – night after night.

This night, waiting for his call, under the dressing of that full-sized bed was no different. I woke up like I had so many nights before. An explosion of energy that crawled through my veins. I would scream and sob, asking God why I was doomed to be alone. The ache deep within my temples made it so hard for me to open my eyes and the light of the moon stung what little vision I could force. There, in the L-shaped bedroom of my parents' home, a home where for so many decades I had known joy, I now knew only agony. The once warm walls stood bare. A single, frill-draped window floated behind the headboard of my full-sized bed and I swam through my tears, waiting for him to call… to come… to care.

Here it was, 2am, and I couldn't get in touch with him. He said that he would call - so that he could come see me; so that he could stay. He promised that he would come lay with me, but his whereabouts, like his intentions, were always a mystery. I was simply a "fill-in" in his polyamorous dramas, where alcohol, drugs and street-life played his leading ladies and real ladies were just distractions from feeling. A slave to the guilt and disappointment of the bad choices and false promises engrained in this affair, I simply waited. I waited for him to call. I waited with excitement, then with angst, then with shame and then, with my longtime companion, loneliness.

We knew each other quite well (by then), loneliness and me. Though, I had no way of forecasting then how powerful a role my relationship with it would come to play. I had yet to discover how strong it was, had no idea of what it was made, why it stalked me, or what it would take for us to one-day part ways. I only knew that it was here now, and while I feared it terribly, I had also come to depend on it quite deeply – the emotional constant in my romantic history – my true love. Loneliness was "The One". The one certainty that I had come to accept, was that we always ended up together… loneliness and I, and it seemed that would never change. I'm not sure why, with all of the great things that I always had going on in my life, was I always so obsessed with the validation that came from a romantic relationship? Why was I sitting there, at 2am, at 23 years old, waiting for this asshole to choose me?

I tried hiding from loneliness this evening, as I had so many nights before, but I was too late. My sea of melancholy had fueled a thunderous storm. Drops of sweat rained down on each crease of the sheets, even as I froze in the cold of winter, shivering with fright and fragility. Tremors traveled from the balls of my feet, through their mid plant, up my ankles and shot like lightning straight into my knees. Then they softly vibrated up. By the time the sensation tangled itself around my spine, I had long resigned to the weight of the sadness it brought with it.

The year was 2003. The movie version of Broadway's big hit "Chicago" had just won an Oscar for Best Picture. Bush announced that he was ready to attack Iraq, without a UN mandate, and 50 Cent's "In Da Club" claimed the year's number one spot on the Billboard charts. I was a twenty-three year old, brown-skinned, curly-haired Latina, living in New York and finishing up my Master's degree in Communications at Fordham University. An educated, attractive, loved young woman in the world's greatest city. I could have been happy. I should have been happy. But was I happy? No… Decidedly, No! In whatever area of my life you picked – career, family, romance – you could find me desperately seeking for some greater sense of fulfillment to bring comfort to my internal sense of isolation. I longed for a deeper connection with someone. Even when among people, I constantly felt a sort of loneliness set in.

I stayed in what became a dangerously abusive relationship with loneliness for years, terrified of its power and still more afraid of its absence. Love story after love story, loneliness remained my constant companion in a series of love-hate triangles where loneliness and I held our ground. The third slot was constantly filled by different love interests who simply cycled through making cameo appearances in this painful threesome. So, goes my story and the years of it that I will share with you here. For, it wasn't until I made peace with being alone almost a decade later, that this loneliness finally exited stage left and the joy of serene solitude began. After feeling the pain, doing the internal work and finding my faith, I finally began to heal.

In the pages that follow lies the story of my love affair with loneliness and my partnership with wellness. It is the story of what happens to a soul when it bonds with an emotion (loneliness) that it also fears (an emotion born of fear itself), and the tale of a heart broken by that union with loneliness. But it is also the story of a courageous search for self that led to challenges and progress, joy and serenity, health and wellness; a story about the will to grow and a developed intolerance for anything less than joy. In each chapter, I share a piece of the pain, passion and power of the experiences that taught me to love myself, God and others. I also share with you the practical ways that you might use these lessons to yield similar outcomes for you.

You'll notice as you read through these pages, the many voices through which this story is told. As the protagonist, I was a broken woman who has now found her way. Simple, really. As the author, however, I am a life coach, a poet, an academic scholar, a spiritual being and your typical Puerto Rican "around the way" girl from New York. Each of those voices creep in and out of the narration you will encounter on this journey. I grew up around both professionals and thugs and sometimes they were one in the same. And while neither my parents nor I were ever directly involved in any of it, I saw and loved my share of folks affected by drugs, jail, homelessness, illiteracy, gangs, abuse, violence and abandonment. I also went to operas and museums, traveled the world and ate truffles at Bloomingdales. I made it my business to see the best and the worst that the world had to offer and didn't blink once – never easily intimidated or easily impressed. I learned early on how to be comfortable around anyone, which meant learning how to shift in and out of multiple worlds. So, just as my experiences have been extremely diverse, so too are my perspectives, my interpretations and even my vernacular.

For instance, I spent years as a performance poet. Spoken word, even in its written form, is still very much a part of my soul. So too, is it a part of this work. Not just in the poetic reflections sprinkled throughout the book, but in some of the flowery descriptions that I deliberately use to color my memories. You'll see the poetry. Yet as much as I am a poet, I am also an academic. So, the seven years that I spent in graduate school pursuing my doctorate, also make a frequent appearance in my way of expressing myself. Despite the faculty's obvious disappointment with never being able to fully acculturate me into the sophisticated scholar that they wished me to be, it wasn't a total loss for them. They still instilled in me a value for research, statistics, facts and scholarly articulation that I may never shake. I dig it. So, I do it.

Then there's the clinical verbiage and advice that was inspired by my training as a mediator, counselor and coach and many years of working in the mental health field. I spent years with folks who discussed diagnoses and disorders, interventions and outcomes, treatment, and trauma. There was a focus on illness and wellness, conflict and peace, joy and sadness and the goal-oriented approach to healing that motivates the "helping" professions. So, I do that too.

That is, when I'm not feeling like my writing is just about taking dictation; at those moments, I write because I must document what I'm feeling being placed into my mind. Sometimes that's the mood. Then, I just type what I get. I write, and it is as if the words are being dropped into my head by some divine source. I don't think about it or strategize the content. As I write, I connect to spirit in some way. Suddenly, I don't necessarily know how I know what I know, or why

I've chosen to phrase it in a particular way: it's so powerful that it has to come through, exactly as it does, and I'm kind of just a stenographer of sorts. So, there's that voice too.

Finally, you'll find that I can also be a bit, what people like to term "urban," whatever that has come to mean. My guess is that it's as close as people can get to calling me Hip Hop without terming me a genre of music. In any event, I grew up in a healthy family in a private house in the suburbs. But yes, I can be a bit "hood." We were lower-middle class which is basically one or two paychecks away from poor. I spent a lot of time with family and friends, in communities of lower socio-economic means. Despite my blessing of a private house in the suburbs, much of my extended family and friends were still pretty engrossed in the culture of contemporary urban poverty – for all of its bad and its good. That made an impact on me. So, you'll find a tinge of that always comes through.

The question has been asked: Which is my true voice? They all are. The many styles of writing that you'll read throughout this work are reflective of the many diverse experiences that live within me and the rollercoaster of expression that codes my style, tone and approach. I am a poetic, academic, claircognizant life coach with a bit of a contemporary urban feel.

As far as the other characters and events described in these chapters – they are truly of my life experience, through my lens as the narrator, with names changed to respect the anonymity of those people referenced. Each of the individuals in this book, regardless of how few or how many sentences are devoted to their description, played an integral part in helping me to face my fears and, in doing so, to reveal my strengths. I have also had many teachers, not mentioned here, whose lessons helped and continue to help me to evolve. It is through that evolution that I came to learn the many tools that I share with you here; tools which I have found helpful on my journey, and which still help guide me today. In that same spirit, as you read this work, may every suggestion that ends a paragraph, every reflection that starts a page, all of the practices that I adopted, thoughts that I challenged and changes I implemented also help you - so that you may continue to access more and more of the truth and beauty within you. After all, all that you seek is already inside.

I know that it may be difficult to believe that you are all that you need and that all that you need to find peace lies within. It sounds very cliché, almost esoteric. I used to feel the same when it was said to me. But let me assure you, as someone who has traveled the world seeking truth and finding beauty, sitting beside many a spiritual teacher, including priests, monks, babalawos (ministers), psychics, and rabbis, that you don't have to go far. I visited world wonders, witnessed healing miracles, communed with nature, and was humbled by joy; and I loved every minute of it. But it was ALONE in a studio apartment in the northeast section of the Bronx, NY that I discovered my truth and beauty: in learning to know and love myself. For it was only in learning to be alone with myself that I could finally break up with loneliness and make peace with solitude. In the peaceful silence of that small residence, staring at a $6 fountain that I bought at Walgreens and a salt lamp that I ordered from Groupon - I finally reclaimed my mind and subsequently my spirit.

That is when I learned that even when you are alone, you are not alone. In fact, I would like you to consider the possibility that when you are the most alone, you are actually the least alone because there are fewer things distracting you from the greatness and grandeur to which you are truly connected. That is why learning to find the peace in being alone became the greatest gift that I ever gave to myself. It taught me to listen to myself and to listen to God by letting myself fully experience the moment, and the more of that listening that I learned to do, the more those two voices started to sound the same. And the more that the self-talk inside of my psyche started to mirror the voice of God energy, of the spiritual universe, the more that I began to trust myself and the world because I was reconnecting to my divinity. It was my greatest entry into profound peace. And that is now the gift that I offer to you—the ability to connect to the divinity inside.

Learning to sit inside yourself, to live inside of yourself, is truly the greatest step to knowing who you are, to enhancing your gifts, to working on your challenges and to loving yourself through the process. And as I have learned, it is possible to love yourself through the process. At first, it's tough to look at everywhere that life has hurt you and find the courage to turn pain into insight, to get up, to push forward and to be happy. I get that. But if you can talk yourself through your fears, find or build your faith and believe in your strengths, quiet your mind and pursue peace, you'll get there. You will get there because it is where you belong, because the only thing holding you back from getting there is you. You deserve peace, you were made from peace and under all the pain you've accumulated sits peace waiting to greet you once more. It was certainly waiting for me.

~ Research & Wrap-Up ~

Of course, I did not always feel like the answers to my sadness were hidden inside my soul. I was once so terrified and tortured by the idea of feeling and being alone. Then, during the writing of this book years later, I discovered, quite ironically, that I was hardly alone in feeling alone. Apparently, the condition of "feeling alone" has, for some time, been at the heart of many a literary work and was the subject of countless sociological and psychological studies. Typically described as either social isolation (the lack of social networks) or emotional isolation (the lack of intimate attachments), loneliness (Weiss, 1973) was the star of many manuscripts, not just my own. Clueless while I was stuck in the experience, I later realized that a cadre of poets, philosophers, gurus, researchers and theorists had dedicated lifetimes to the study of my friend and nemesis: loneliness. It was a club that I had reluctantly joined. Now, paying my membership dues in cold sweats and dark cries, I applaud their efforts, for I know their plights well, and marvel at their insights.

For me, initially at least, emotional isolation had become the heartbeat of my evenings. I craved feeling romantically connected, in an intimate way, to someone. And the fear of not achieving that closeness, had become my "boogey man." It was the monster under my bed, candy man - my proverbial poltergeist. And a busy monster, it was. You see, it turns out that the fear of being alone is, in fact, quite prevalent. One study that looked at how people felt about being alone, found that 99.7% of people surveyed (153), claimed they would feel worthless if alone, feared being alone because of the negative judgment of others or simply feared: spinsterhood, not having a long-term companion, growing old alone, or never having children and a family. A small percentage of that group even said that any relationship, even a horrible one, was better than not being in one at all (Spielmann, 2013). So, who exactly was it that said, "better to be alone than be in bad company?" And better yet...who did they say it to; because very few were listening.

It appears that even in this time of independence, in America with its culture of individuality, being alone still triggers the fears of even the most independent souls. Who truly knows why? I imagine it has something to do with the vulnerability we feel in solitude - naked to the world (and to ourselves). It's as if our greatest insecurities become exposed -

no one to hide behind, no one to blame, no one to ask, no one to learn from - the greatest exercise in self-acceptance (or not). Maybe it is because, as social beings, we long for connection. Perhaps our existence finds validation in the eyes of others because we hope they might reveal our value and without that we are left to wonder indefinitely about our worth. Who knows?

There are many scientific debates about what causes feelings of loneliness. Experts call what made me cry, the theory of cognitive discrepancy. At its core, it focuses on the stress people feel when they think about their life and find that it is dramatically different from what they had expected (Peplau & Perlman, 1982). That was me - constantly obsessed with thoughts of how my love and happiness "should" look and how different that was from the mess I had created. Similarly, I would sit and think about who I "should" be and how that wasn't who I was. My "actual self" was so disconnected from my thoughts of who my "ideal self" was, that I felt defeated and depressed. I was suffering from more than cognitive discrepancy (a mismatch of thoughts) -- I was suffering from self-discrepancy - a mismatch of selves (Kuperschmidt, 1999). And at the heart of it all, pulling the strings, was loneliness.

Little by little my loneliness would worsen into anxiety and depression as it is likely to do (Cacioppo, 2006) and I would become paralyzed by a stinging sensation that left my spirit, my soul in pain and my body frozen. Days would pass with me having accomplished nothing which only created a sense of hopelessness and shame. With each frozen moment came a feeling of having done less work, in the world and on myself. That led to feeling worthless and thus, feeling worthy of less. Oh, how I wish that I could have handled it differently - had better skills, more insight or the courage to snap out of it. I wish I would have tried appreciating what I had (blessings in abundance - food, shelter, family) instead of focusing on what I didn't have (known as "adaptation"). I wish that I knew enough to change the objects of my obsessive thoughts, or to maybe spend more time doing things that I enjoy doing alone (known as "task choice"), like meditating, sketching, journaling, crocheting, writing, reading. I wish that I would have rethought my criteria for what relationships looked like so that I sought out healthy and happy instead of needy and fleeting (known as "changed standards"). The truth is that the productive possibilities for how I could have managed my loneliness were endless (Peplau & Perlman, 1981); still, I chose to suffer instead. It seemed like the only option available at the time, because it came so naturally. It was the only one I knew.

When combatting negative feelings of loneliness, we professionals suggest improving your social skills (e.g. developing better communication skills), enhancing social supports (e.g. building networks), increasing opportunities for social contact (e.g. changing calendar activities), and changing the unhealthy and unhelpful thoughts in your head (Masi, 2010). Want to know how the "me" of then handled it, though? I went with good old-fashioned crying, obsessing, yelling, screaming, questioning life, hating God, and ultimately, doubting my purpose. There's just something about the classics.

Then one day, exhausted and determined, something clicked in my spirit. I knew I had to change. I worked at it until tears gave way to laughter and laughter gave way to love... self-love. Though unaware of it at the time, my path to healing led me through the eight dimensions of wellness (Swarbrick, 2006). For, I had been literally love-sick, and it was now time to get well. It was time to take the time and energy that I had for so long dedicated to men, and redirect them toward myself. It was time to change, how I thought, how I felt and what I did. Interestingly enough, I came to find that being alone provided the perfect opportunity for me to do just this. Loneliness was no longer my enemy. I understood it as a feeling that I could process and then let go. And in that letting go, I learned to be happy when I was alone, and solitude became my friend. I created multiple self-care practices in each dimension of wellness: emotional, financial, social, spiritual, occupational, physical, intellectual and environmental. In each, I worked my thoughts, processed my feelings, and modified my behavior. In each, I developed at least three habits that fulfilled me and the truth of who I am. Through these steps, I learned how to love myself, truly; how to make each thought, feeling and behavior in my life, consistent and aligned with self-love. I learned how to redirect my time and energy toward self so that I might be whole, happy, healthy and healed. That's what I now share with you.

To be clear, this is my story, my personal journey and as such, I do not pretend to provide universal answers here. In fact, if I have any hope for this book at all, it is that you walk away from it asking questions you've never been brave enough to ask, with the tools you need to actively go out into the world and dig deep into yourself in search of your answers. Make the hard choices, sit in discomfort, question the negative thought patterns, dance in the park, journal at night, try a yoga pose at work during a break or simply commit to smiling more. Ask why, look deeper, travel far, let others get close, set limits in love, accept no limits in life and connect to nature. Find your joy! In the experience of that search will be the brilliance of enlightenment... the understanding that at its best, the quest for spiritual harmony lies not in any answer, but in the courage to perpetually question, free from a need for answers, satisfied with the beauty of the question itself, fulfilled by the pursuit, and gratified by humble curiosity.

... Now, walk with me, as we travel back to my pain, and then through to my peace!

Poetic Reflection: Loneliness

It never felt like enough ... To be at peace, to reach happiness, to deserve love
Instead it was chilly inside and life always felt more like a compromise to avoid the lonely nights of cries that would surely come to characterize my life if I didn't transform into whoever they thought I was... or needed me to be
It never felt safe to just be me
The stinging observations of childhood critics had been tattooed on my self-esteem
And the chameleon I became to try to meet everyone else's needs became so isolated from my dreams that the vision of who I truly wanted to become just seemed to lose priority
I just wanted to be accepted, life became about not feeling lonely
And then romance became about not feeling lonely, and then because love can be so tricky, not feeling lonely became nothing more than a fantasy
Why can't I just be free?
As loneliness came to decorate the days and nights of my reality I found myself confronted by the realization that in loneliness silence was loud, thoughts were imprisoning, and someone had hidden the key... to my liberation
Loneliness turned to sadness turned to frustration
If I could just learn to take control of the internal conversations, then maybe being alone wouldn't be so scary
Maybe it wouldn't be so bad to be left alone with myself...
Maybe I might even find the beauty...

Part I

Them

❧

Men
&
My Many Affairs
With Loneliness

Through Our
LATINA LENS

Este Amor Pertenece A Una Novela

In 1992, Salsa music superstar Tito Rojas, released the track, "Porque Este Amor" (Because This Love). The song's hook, "Porque este amor pertenece a una novela" (because this love belongs in a Spanish soap opera), instantly resonated with almost every Latino listener, skyrocketing it to the top of the charts. Why? Because most of us were raised watching novelas and knew exactly what he was describing: the drama, the passion, the high highs and low lows.   I remember sitting between my abuela and abuelo on our brown, corduroy reclining love seat, watching, "Topacio." It was the story of a poor, blind orphan, who gets courted by and married to a rich heir. For 181 episodes, we're entangled in an epic and tragic love story involving manipulative villains, a fake rape, a swapped-at-birth reveal and an eventual happy ending.

Sound familiar? Of course, it does, mostly because it's reminiscent of another fan favorite - 1970's "Esmeralda". But that's because who can resist stories about a blind orphan girl, switched at birth? In fact, similarly outlandish storylines ran through many of Spanish television's nightly novelas, but it didn't matter because we still watched them all. We were addicted to the drama - the long passionate kisses, the long-swing slaps; the convoluted relationships, the "meant to be" love with the "meant to be hard" lives. The tragic suffering with some magical happy ending, the big lies that led to big reveals, betrayal and redemption, all normalized and consumed night after night. Now, I know fairytales and reality shows have had similar effects on other women, but this, right here, was the special brand of romantic crazy that they fed us Latinas. Sure, it was meant to be entertaining and entertaining it was... but one might wonder if it also conditioned us to tolerate, if not expect, a special brand of crazy in our relationships?

It's hard to look at the romances in my 20s without surmising that I had certainly become addicted to drama, tolerant of crazy and comfortable with a convoluted storyline of suffering and lies in the name of a possible happy ending...

Mr. Marmalade Skin

We had come to know each other quite intimately over the years, loneliness and I. That feeling of emptiness that being alone brings was like darkness being fed through my veins. It haunted me with its useless weight and painful memories, never coming up from behind its own shadows, and still somehow always powerful enough to make me feel small inside. Ours was a long-time, irresistible attraction. In retrospect, I'm not quite sure if it was really strong or if I was just really weak. Either way, loneliness and I were definitely a vibrational match to one another – the perfect fit. And when I left for college, well… that's when our affair really got hot and heavy.

See, in 1998, I decided to "go away" to school, which meant 45 minutes from my parents' home in Yonkers, NY to the town of Hempstead, Long Island. Hofstra University was a closed campus with a safe walk through gardens and over small pedestrian bridges leading to classroom buildings. It was close enough for me to get back home quickly if I needed to, but far enough for me to claim to be "on my own." Their housing was nice. The suites were mostly occupied by athletes and the children of higher income brackets. My dorm room, on the other hand, was in the towers. There, bathrooms were shared with the rest of the floor and living spaces were a bit smaller. I was on a partial scholarship and living in a "double" room in *Constitution Hall* (a co-ed high-rise). My roommate and I were best friends from high school, which made the transition to living "alone" much easier – particularly since I wasn't actually alone at all. Still, it was my first time away from home and there were many days, and many more nights, when alone was exactly what I felt.

I did date and party – just not a lot of it. Unlike a few of my peers who went crazy the minute that they were out of their parents' reach, I was no stranger to freedom. I had a fairly liberal but supportive upbringing so being unsupervised carried little novelty. Plus, I was serious about my education. I wanted to be the first of my immediate family members to graduate college. It was important to me. Which meant that my grades were important too, and a social life... not so much. That is of course, until Mr. Marmalade Skin strolled in.

We clicked almost immediately, him and me. The tone of his complexion, the way he smelled, even the taste of his kiss – all reminiscent of honey with a tinge of something zesty. Slender, tall, with a smile that would not retreat. He was a junior, philosophy major, a rapper, I think – lived in the building of a new best friend of mine. As luck would have it, I was on a work-study assignment that sat me in the "security" booth of various campus residences, collecting IDs, signing people in and buzzing doors. Sometimes, it put me in their building on night shifts that ushered in daylight. I mostly used the time to study and read; I really wasn't interested in a boyfriend, but he was so sweet, and funny, too. His coming home during my twilight shifts should have been a warning to me, but he was so charming. And I was so naïve. We were a match made in purgatory.

It started with a few "How you doing" looks as he made his way through the doors of *Enterprise Hall*. Soon, looks turned to those half smiles that help your eyes flirt. A few compliments followed. In just a matter of weeks, we were friendly. Then there were long phone conversations, winter walks to class and "movie nights" that went later and later. Before I knew it, I couldn't stand to be away from him. I jumped into his arms when I saw him walking toward me. He spun me in the air, holding me tight and all I could think was: "so, this is why everyone's so into this love shit." A warm chill would shoot up my thighs, through my torso and into my lungs. That same chill seemed to then paint a grin on my face that it pushed right out of my pupils. I was elated—my soul filled with so much paradise, my heart racing. Finally, I understood the world's obsession with romance; the way everyone surrendered to its majesty. I, too, wanted it to change me, needed it to last. Everything seemed so manageable with it; nothing too big to tackle.

With that sort of inspiration, fun days turned to months of excitement in bliss. It felt so fulfilling and life was so enjoyable. I just knew that our love could withstand anything. Or at least, that's what I hoped. That's what I hoped when his ex-girlfriend called and said that she was five months pregnant, two months into our relationship. That's what I hoped when she called four months later to assure me that he would be hers one day, once more. That's what I hoped when I heard the rumors of other girls, when he shut me out because he didn't "feel like dealing with things," when he drank, when he got high, when he ignored me.

That was definitely what I convinced myself of as I cried myself to sleep almost a year later. I couldn't bear to believe that, little by little, Mr. Marmalade Skin had become less and less interested in me – the one to whom he professed his love, his "queen." Though, when I come to think of it, who could blame him? After all, hadn't I become less and less interested in myself; preoccupied only with his needs – with making sure that his debt was paid off, that his daughter was well taken care of, that his insecurities were never triggered? With all of the drama constantly at his feet, we both subconsciously behaved as if my needs were no longer on the agenda of this relationship; instead it was all always about him. And under the rules of that unspoken agreement lived some of the saddest years of my life, some of the loneliest.

The first adult relationship that I ever experienced, and I was lost in romantic chaos. I believed everything he said: that he didn't know that girl, that he and that other girl were just friends, that he didn't go to that party, that he loved no one else but me, that he needed to take a walk (for four hours) to clear his head. I mean, why wouldn't I believe him? I was giving my all. I loved him so much and he knew that to his core. I could think of no reason for why he would lie, not to me. Even when that little knot in my stomach said, "something is off," I refused to believe that he could betray me. I needed to believe him... So, I did; against all reason. Despite what my mother warned, and my dad hinted; against the odds my friends predicted and the pinch in my gut – I believed him. I chose his side of arguments. I supported his stories of how he was always the victim – in his childhood, in past romances, in the world.

I never questioned his capacity to love. I never examined his ability to commit. I simply handed myself over – heart and soul – whatever he needed. I charged his daughter's clothes on my credit card at Macy's. I begged for family favors, so he'd have shelter when he was kicked off campus with nowhere to go. I moved dorm rooms so that he could stay with me. I encouraged his every childhood dream of becoming a chef. I made plans to relocate with him to make that feasible. I reignited his goals. I renegotiated mine – what I wanted to study, where I wanted to live, what kind of intimacy I really hoped for in a relationship. I re-envisioned and re-conceptualized my life to fit his lies. I believed him. I believed in him! Not only did I believe that he loved me, I believed that one day that love could feel good again.

After all, I was no innocent victim, here. I loved and believed him because I needed to. I loved him... for me. I believed him for me – because I couldn't be alone, because I had risked everything to be his, because I needed to be right, because I could change him, because I couldn't start over, because I wasn't going to let "those people" win. I wasn't going prove right the many friends and family members that doubted our strength as a couple. So, you see, I suffered not at his hands, but at the mercy of my fearful beliefs - because I wanted to love him the way that I wanted to love him and not even he was going to make me reconsider that (my stubborn neediness). I did not understand it then, but the one hurting me was me, because I just could not leave and leave him be. Instead, I pushed harder.

Meanwhile, his once consistent sleeping habits turned to cameo appearances in our bed. First, he came home really late. Then he didn't come home at all, then two nights in a row... then three... and enter Loneliness! All at once a rush through my diaphragm – the scent of rejection and bitter taste of disloyalty would begin to consume me. I would call and get no answer. I would adore, with no reciprocation. Loneliness and I would wait up together, obsessing with no relief. When Mr. Marmalade would finally arrive, there was only rage and bargaining. He blamed me for pushing him away. I blamed him for the deceit and the disregard. He promised to change, to stay, and never to leave me alone with my fears for that long again. I promised to forgive, forget, try to move forward without holding on to the pain; and we would. Though, that usually held up for only a few weeks. Then we would get close, I would smother to keep him close, I imagine he would get scared and *she* would get more attractive.

I believe on some level that I always knew that he was cheating. It was just so hard to face—so hard to consider that the first man to whom I gave my all could ultimately be so

31

unimpressed by me that he would seek out another. I mean, I had dated before him, sure. But never had I invested so much of who I was; never had I made a spoken commitment to try everything to make a monogamous, long-term relationship work, until now. This was a "first." And on many levels, I think I wanted to believe that this could be the last; that this kind of work only had to be experienced once in life, with one partner, for one "happily ever after" to be "earned."

Until then, I always fancied myself a cynic, too clever to believe in "happily-ever-after" – that is, until I felt the possibility with him. Then all bets were off. I never imagined that my affair with Mr. Marmalade would end with me in the arms of loneliness. I had come to know loneliness at some points throughout my childhood, but I thought adulthood would be different; romance would be different. This romance had to be different. I thought if I just stuck with it, it would work – that I could "fix" it. And so, began my fantasy that if I loved someone enough, my love could change them: undo childhood traumas, change his hurtful behavior, help him learn to love me in a way that felt better; that if I was patient, Marmalade would finally, truly, see me, and consequently, see the best of himself. So, I ignored the ways he hurt me, held on in the hopes that he would ultimately fulfill his promised devotion to me, kept on loving him and made believe *she* didn't exist.

The rumors came by the dozens in phone calls and visits from friends. I just brushed them off. I explained away my anxieties, with stories I told myself to minimize the angst. "He likes to take long walks to clear his head," I told myself, and others. "He's got a lot on his plate and sometimes he just needs some 'man' time with his cousin." "He's doing the best that he can, with intimacy. It was never his thing, but he's trying for me." I was truly talented at scripting his defense...
And then I found out that I knew her.

32

She was a friend of a friend that I had met a few times. The news hit me with the force of a punch to the chest that left me breathless. It was a dreaded realization: now, I would have to confront the longtime suspicion. No more blowing it off. No more hiding behind alleged uncertainty. Marmalade and his mistress had now been seen together and in the court of public opinion it was ruled that I was no longer allowed to ignore this. It was clearly time to make some difficult choices. I would have to take a position on my own happiness. Or at least that's what others were telling me. So, I did what I felt socially compelled to do. I addressed it. With pleas for honesty and tears to camouflage the anger, I approached each of them separately: "I'm asking you respectfully, to tell me the truth about your friendship... is it romantic... have you dated, kissed, slept together... are you seeing one another... just please be honest... are you having an affair?" They both denied it. She claimed outrage. Marmalade called me crazy. They swore that it was a misunderstanding. That their friendship was just that a friendship.

"Whew," I thought. And just like that, I was willing to let it go. I was happy to be off the hook of having to change my life because of it! I could now hurry up and get back to the comfort of my illusion. It was so difficult to even *think* about starting over with someone else, let alone creating a *plan* to do so, and forget about the actual moving forward and execution! Plus, I believed, wholeheartedly, that if I held on a little longer, he would wake up one day and see how amazing I was, how much I loved him, how wrong he had been and how happy we could be. So, I held on. And the more patient I was, the better I tried to love him, the more he escaped, running away until running was all he knew how to do. A habit. A constant. And always, there to clean up the mess was good old reliable loneliness – tugging at tear ducts and soothing the burn of betrayal with the cold of emptiness.

Things between me and Marmalade were a roller coaster of highs and lows for two years. For a while towards the end, things were great. I offered an ultimatum some weeks prior that if the sun ever beat him home again, I would leave. It was now the Spring of my sophomore year and a transfer was attractive for both financial and emotional reasons. That transfer would take me back to Westchester and I wanted him to join me. I wasn't sure exactly how, but I knew that we could make it work. In the weeks that followed, that ultimatum tucked him into bed alongside me every night and I was sure that the nightmare was over, certain that he finally realized what this could be and that he had committed to it fully. We were talking engagement and a family one day; moving far away. He was to attend culinary school. I was to pursue a career in public relations at a nearby university. We would grow old together, become successful together, and build a future together. I was not only hopeful; I was full of eagerness for tomorrow.

So, imagine my reaction one night, when hours passed with no return, after his leaving for the store at 9pm. Around 10pm, I thought to myself, "You just need to trust him." By 11pm, I was thinking, "You just need to call him." When the clock struck midnight, I began to think, "You may need to kill him." Finally, at 3am, my best friend answered my panicked phone call by coming down to babysit me for hours as I contemplated everything from suicide to homicide. Of course, to her, it was obvious where he had gone and who he was with. I'm sure that it's even obvious to you. Me, however, I just refused to believe that he could knowingly hurt me again—not after how well we were doing, not after how much of myself I had sacrificed, not knowing that he could permanently lose me (assuming of course that he believed my ultimatum at all; that either of us did). My shaking had given way to sheer exhaustion by the time that she finally began to call hospitals and morgues. I had assured her that they were stronger possibilities than the bed of some other woman. After all, he couldn't be out cheating on me, not again. In disbelief and disillusionment, each one of my tears chased out the other and every cry used more and more of my oxygen until the lessening gasps of hope drained my faith. I will admit that I lost some trust in God that day. I believe "anxiety" is what they call it. I lapsed into despair, finally closing my swollen eyes at approximately 6:30am to seek solace in the pseudo-sleep that awaited me. Then, around 8ish, got dressed and went to class. I was still an "A" student and this changed nothing. Plus, it was all I could do not to break down.

Mid-afternoon, I returned from "Introduction to Philosophy," to find Mr. Marmalade Skin taking sanctuary in one of his safest of refuges (our bed). Secure in the love that I always offered, he began to rant and rave about what I had done, yet again, to make him need to run away. He blamed me – something I said that he initially ignored had grown to upset him. He claimed that I pushed too hard and made him stay away. It was classic; it was me – my fault. I was too emotionally exhausted to fight it with any real insight. I was angry and hurt. But mostly I was numb and vulnerable. We argued and accused each other of things. There was crying and softness. Then, demands were made. We later laid in silence visited by stares of contempt. Soon, we were back at it again. Connected in our fear, we walked away in our hearts and just yelled in rage. Kisses would interrupt to remind us of moments lost. Then, like clockwork, we would begin to enact the resentment we had come to feel for our love. We held on to gripping fingertips and incessant pride. Pointing fingers were internalized. Our egos engaged their greatest defenses. Then, as it was to be, we broke up and he moved out.

As you might guess, left to keep me company was loneliness – to lay on my chest, to play picture slide shows in my dreams, to point out the many things that I could have done differently, to linger. So we got close, loneliness and I; lots of cleaning, long walks, longer nights. We were already pretty good friends given Marmalade's many prior escapades, but this time, it would go much longer. Or so I thought, until Mr. Marmalade Skin returned weeks later with promises that it would be different. It didn't take much pleading for him to convince me again. He just apologized, and I caved. Not out of love for him, but out of the fear that it could end up being just me and loneliness for years. Let's be honest here, for as close as loneliness and I were getting, I was still afraid of its piercing hollowness and bitter company. Marmalade was unreliable, but loneliness was inconsolable. And there's that whole, "the evil you know" adage. I thought it better to take my chances with Marmalade and see where it goes.

It was months before his actions once again reminded me that we were still going nowhere. This time, however, I was already living back home with family and friends who truly loved me, and had done so for years, in a way that felt great to my spirit. I had begun to remember what love – the kind of love that I wanted – really felt like. And in the brilliance provided by that contrast, I lost interest in the taste of Marmalade. It was now the summer of 2000 and I had finally found the courage to walk away from the toxicity of his charm. It would be just the two of us after all, just me and loneliness once more.

Mr. Caramel Eyes

The fall of 2000 ushered in a dry-spell for me and loneliness. Though it visited on occasion, our rendezvous were few and far between. Still back in my childhood home, I had reconnected with the safety and security from which I had always drawn confidence. My academic transfer was official, and I was now also working for an internet stock company. From 10am to 6pm, I was their administrative assistant and then it was off to class from 7pm to 10pm. Sure it was hard to stay up to all hours of the night studying but I was making more than any of my friends; a full-time salary with benefits and bonuses at 20 years old – and that was just the start. I loved my pencil skirts and high heels, plus I was paying part of the mortgage, not to mention the independence that seemed to just grow exponentially with every month that passed. First, I spent a few weekends in Puerto Rico, then a week in London. Suddenly I was going out of town four or five times, per year, on getaways and road trips.

My first car was a midnight blue 2002 Honda Civic EX with a sunroof. It may not seem like much to you, but it was EVERYTHING to me; independence and freedom. It was my tour guide through every hip hop and Salsa club that New York City had to offer. It escorted me on long weekends away and on every date, I could fit in between. I was living life and loving every second of it. Before I knew it, undergrad was through and I was onto my Master's degree in Public Communications at Fordham University - nine months of intense coursework, practicums, mentorships and lots of writing. Let's see, there was an internship at ABC news, one at MTV Networks and soon I was writing for Urban Latino Magazine. I was 23, interviewing politicians, partying with celebrities and putting the insights of every encounter in black on white for publication.

The world was my oyster. Or so it seemed. That is, until the summer of 2003 when school ended, and the career search began. All of a sudden, all bets were off. I can't explain it. It was as if my well of luck had gone dry. I went on interviews for television jobs, applied for teaching gigs and pursued leads for a writing career – nothing! What modeling jobs I could secure were more exploitative than lucrative. Every which way I turned, the road led to disappointment. To say that I was in the midst of an existential crisis would be a drastic understatement. I felt like nothing could go right. I felt like my life was in shambles. I was unemployed for the first time since age 11, out of school for the first time since age 5 and doors just kept slamming in my face. The future was uncertain, and I felt useless, worthless and lost. With my purpose foggy, my talent felt arbitrary. I became reckless. My familial relationships were strained by my lying and emotional distance. Love was empty. Even my faith had started to fade. The more prayers that felt unanswered, the angrier I became with God, and the more disappointed I became with life. And the more rejection I experienced, the lonelier my existence.

Lost, I began to connect with individuals whose days were just as empty and lonely—they had time to waste and attention to spare. During 2003, I met and spent time with some of the smartest, sweetest, most genuinely good-hearted, fun, and talented individuals you ever want to know. They also had some of the deepest wounds, worst insecurities, dimmest pasts and most destructive habits I've witnessed. But let's face it, I wasn't faring much better. It was an era of darkness for me too, fueled by dark liquors that hazed my dark nights. I slept through most mornings, my eyes closed to the light—in so many ways. There were blessings in abundance, but I couldn't see them then. All I saw were slights – places where fate had cheated me. Loneliness had come back to stay, and I so badly wanted to find a way to force it out, in whatever way I could.

Then, because the universe has a sense of humor, I met Mr. Caramel Eyes. His kiss was the perfect blend of passion fruit and whiskey: sweet and numbing. It was as if hope had run to take shelter in his eyes: there was just something about the match of their tone to his skin's caramel-colored melanin that reminded me of how perfect we all are—a divine sketch. I was inspired. How could I not be when even his flaws seemed beautiful in the sun's light? The problem with Mr. Caramel Eyes was that he had a girlfriend...and she wasn't me! She was the very reason I stayed away at first – their baby was to be born in a few months and despite his stories of separate sleeping arrangements and promises of platonic co-parenting, I just was not interested.

This was a line in the sands of karma that I promised myself that I would never cross; a pain that I swore I would never inflict on another person. After all, it was a pain with which I was all too familiar. My many nights of suffering over Mr. Marmalade had tattooed upon my spirit a certain moral code, a pledge of compassion that strengthened my resolve with every tear that fell on the university-issued twin bed of my college dorm. On those nights when I most questioned my value, I also most strongly committed to my values—I would never be her! It was all I could hold onto in those moments of loneliness and fear, the judgment that I was better and didn't deserve this; the idea, certainty even, that no woman would ever cry because her man was with me. I never knowingly dated men who were involved. I knew the paralysis of getting caught in that web, and it was not for me. This was no different. And the pregnant girlfriend was far from the worst of it. There were other girls, and drugs, an unsteady income, even some gang stuff. You describe a father's worst nightmare and Caramel Eyes pretty much exemplified it.

I thanked Mr. Caramel Eyes for his compliments during our first meeting early 2003, trying not to look into his eyes. They contained all the pain of an abandoned child grown to be a man full of broken dreams. His looks were both so piercing and inviting, all at once. Proud of my conviction, intrigued by his energy and uninterested in his drama, I walked away. It was difficult. But at the end of the day, I felt good about who I was and that is a priceless experience—to lay your head on a pillow at night feeling peace with how your spirit interacted with other spirits on that day. I had decided that peace of mind was all I needed. No need for caramel.

And then one summer day he called me, claiming that a mutual friend had passed on my number. Our families had been friends for decades. It was easy to believe. He began professing his need to have me in his life, explaining away the relationship with his girlfriend as "just a living situation" that he could not yet get out of because of the baby that was on the way. His tone had such an honest quality to it. His plea felt so legitimate. And that day, I felt my walls lose some strength...no matter how much bull-crap I knew I was being fed. If you could just hear the tenderness of his speech, you might sympathize. When he asked me to teach him how to love, I melted a little. He insisted that my taking an interest in him was all he needed to access a piece of himself that he had long ago locked away – a way to be vulnerable again, to be open. He spoke of abandonment that had turned to fear and disappointment that had turned to hopelessness and spoke of a friendly relationship where I might help him learn to be soft again. I had never seen manipulation and sincerity operating in tandem. This was my first time.

Still, I kept my cool and refused to engage. Not only was another woman involved, who deserved respect and compassion, but she was pregnant! There was a life coming, a life deserving the opportunity of a family unit, a life whose earliest familial memories would be impacted by how I handled this very situation; a bond that would potentially keep Mr. Caramel Eyes eternally connected to her. And although they had issues of their own that would probably drive them apart, I didn't need to be the cause, the excuse or the distraction.

I avoided him and moved forward. I kept my distance from family functions that he might attend. I engaged only in the smallest of courteous talk when our paths did cross. I did my due diligence to create a space between us, despite his wishes. My morals kept me focused for a while. But soon it seemed like he was everywhere that I went. We just kept "bumping into each other" more and more and the courteous banter grew longer and longer. Before I knew it, we were friends - really just friends: long philosophical conversations about faith and politics, music, poetry, comedy, fun; completely platonic. Then, the conversations developed into lunches and dinner parties at the houses of mutual friends. Soon, we were spending every day together—amusement parks, walks on the beach, his musical performances, shopping—everything became an opportunity to spend time together. We debated political points of view, overlapped laughs, spoke our most intimate truths—stories about the pain his father left behind, the silence his mother caused, the things he wished he could change. I went on about the dreams I couldn't let go of, the things that I felt the world owed me, the scared little girl who needed validation. The trust built so quickly; the connection felt so otherworldly. Soon evening events were added to the regular routine, which led to midnight dinner dates and watching the sun come up. Everyone could see what was coming...including him. I seemed to be the only one interested in the delusion that this was platonic. Little by little the lines began to blur. Our "best friend"-ship quickly turned to more—more heat, more heaven, more headaches and more heartache.

It was exciting in the beginning as I imagine are most affairs. There was chemistry and cognitive compatibility, challenges and aspirations, a promise for a new beginning. For better or worse, we were falling in love. And despite all the reasons it may have been morally wrong, emotionally, it couldn't have felt more right. Every touch of his rough, callused hands sparked the sharpest quiver through my chest cavity: my breath, paralyzed; my reason, held hostage; my attention, arrested. I swear I felt a little less concerned with the world while wrapped inside the negligent bliss of his caress. What a comforting cocoon it was. No matter how tight or how fleeting, it was warmth in its most pure form. Without it, everything seemed to hurt. With it, everything else seemed to stop. Others ceased to matter. Time failed to pass. Rain evaporated as it fell. Even birds postponed their flights, so as not to miss us while we kissed. The rest of the city seemingly paused to listen to our love, or at least to act as the backdrop to our little romantic adventure. And for every standstill in motion of things around us, my heart would beat just a little quicker, my pulse just a little faster.

That is, until our egos showed their faces—his jealousy, my rage. It was hard not to let them in. They just kept knocking on the doors of our uncertainties, getting stronger and stronger as our obsession with one another grew deeper and deeper. My guilt and shame turned to insecurity and, soon, paranoia. His fears enmeshed with his desire made him distant and controlling. Neither one of us was truly sure that we could really trust the other. So, we fought constantly to keep the hold we had over one another. He would stay for nights at a time and then ignore me for days on end. The more I demanded that he change, the more steadfastly he held onto his habits. The more that he asked that I go out on a limb for him, the more of my support I would retract. He couldn't leave. I couldn't breathe. We had begun to play "who can piss the other person off the most." And that turned into "who can cause the most pain." And that, well, that's the last game we ever played together. We got so good at it that we beat each other. Right out of love. Right out of health.

That's the harmful thing about a relationship where there are no rules...THERE ARE NO RULES! Certain roles, like that of a girlfriend, come with a prescribed social expectation. But the word "mistress" only comes with stigma, horror, shame and guilt. I wasn't his girlfriend because he already had a girlfriend. And with the stigma, horror, shame and guilt of what we were doing hanging over our love, we couldn't pull it together to be clear about what we wanted, deserved or would accept. We felt we had no right to place expectations on something that we shouldn't even be doing. So instead, we just did whatever we could to be with one another. And in those moments when we couldn't be together, we did everything we could to cope with the longing...sweet phone calls to express the love, harassing phone calls to demand more time, alcohol to numb the pain, attention in the eyes of other admirers. I sank deeper into my depression. He sank deeper into his arrogance. As I tended to do, I turned to poetry, sadness and attitude. He turned to other women, illicit substances and music. More than anything, I wanted him to choose me. More than anything, he wanted to believe that a choice would never be forced upon him. He promised that with more time and more of my patience would come a resolution, a cleansing of the betrayal, a new day. And I wanted to believe him with every ache in my soul. I think he did, too, but no one wins in a love that selfish. I wanted him at all costs. And he, well, he wanted it all.

I'm not sure if he was addicted to me or to the high he got from seeing me addicted to him, but either way, we craved each other's attention, thrived in the warmth of our private moments, repented internally during the public moments, and hungered for what it could have been if we each weren't so poisoned by what it actually was. He was so wounded. I was so lost. Maybe if his father hadn't... Maybe if his mother would have... Maybe he could have trusted his potential, believed in others, grown to choose love over fear... Maybe if the world hadn't been so cold to him, maybe warmth wouldn't have scared him, made him mean, maybe love could have lived inside of us. And maybe if my dad was more... Or my mom less... Maybe I would have been different. Less ambitious. More peaceful. Maybe if my world could have been more tranquil, maybe we could have been. We lived and loved only in a world of maybes.

I became consumed with impossibilities, each one further confirming for me what I suspected most in this time of depression: that I wasn't really worth loving. As I think back on it, there was clearly a reason that I stayed. Few of us are ever really victims; most of the time we're getting something out of it, on some level, whether we can admit it or not. And I realize that it fit so perfectly with the way that I truly felt about myself at the time and the story that I was telling myself about who I was and what kind of world I occupied. I was insecure, afraid and convinced that I was unworthy of more. With everything falling apart around me, more than ever, I felt utterly unlovable. And this relationship not only confirmed that sad story, it gave me someone to blame for it—someone other than myself. It was perfect!

One day, I got a call from him saying that he was going to try to make it work with the mother of his newborn. I should have been enraged. Given, our enmeshment, I should have felt betrayed… determined to fight. Instead, I felt released – relieved from duty. We had broken up and reconciled several times by now; each separation more painful than the last; each reunion a little steamier. But this time was different. I could feel it deep down in my soul. The writing had been written on the wall the night of our first kiss, and we were finally learning to read. Too much pain had been inflicted. No viable reparations could restore what we had destroyed. I applauded his decision and ended the call with a deep exhale. It had been 18 months since the courting began and 12 months since I had given in. Already the damage was befitting lifetimes of war. These were losses that had to be cut; and so, they were.

I cried nights on end, begging for God's forgiveness for the mess that we had made and remembering the times we shared. Our love was the quintessential romantic tragedy complete with intensity, passion, power and the demise of its protagonists all wrapped in two winters and a spring. Neither he nor I could deny the inevitable reality – in our quest to come together, we had each fallen apart.

Mr. Cinnamon Smile

I had barely recovered from the calamity of my caramel addiction, when I was accepted into Fordham University's PhD program in Sociology. Now the summer of 2004, I was just beginning to put the pieces of my life back together. Several temp job placements finally gave way to a semi-permanent assignment at a pharmaceutical company. I was tasked with developing databases and handling other administrative duties. Doctoral courses began that September. My parents and I were repairing the trust I shattered with my selfish saga of secrets and lies and silly alibies, and I was finally starting to breathe again.

Little by little I had begun to convince myself that life was worth living even if living the life that I had long envisioned for myself might not be possible. It was time for a "Plan B." I had to pick myself up and get from under the depths of that depression – that feeling of uselessness, hopelessness and heaviness that I was carrying around. I had to get up every morning and go somewhere where my work was valued. I had to come home and rebuild with the people who most mattered. I had to pursue this degree because it would open more doors, not just for me but for those I could help with the knowledge I'd attain. And most importantly, I needed to make peace with loneliness because we were about to give our relationship another shot!

By the Fall, things were going well. I had filled a few notepads with profound poetry and inspired art. I was reading and re-reading some pretty eye opening new age books. I was in therapy and prayer groups, and I was smiling. It was taking all of me, but I was healing. A poet friend of mine got me a consulting gig doing empowerment work with young women in D.C. on the weekends. When I wasn't engrossed in that, I was back in the clubs. Life was fun again. I dated an athlete or two, joined a pageant I'd heard about, did some more modeling, got some freelance writing work with a few magazines and sought out a therapist. The energy that I used to channel, was once again starting to flow.

I also did a lot of praying - to a God that I only partially believed in - for a love that could feel good to my soul. This "God" had proven to be unreliable in the past so, I wasn't getting my hopes up, but I figured that it was worth the ask. Time passed, and bad dates were coming a mile a minute. Imagine my surprise when, there he was, exactly what I prayed for: my knight in shining armor - everything that Mr. Caramel and Marmalade weren't. He was all that I had prayed to God for: single, straight, smart, sexy, educated and sweet, with a good sense of humor and a strong moral compass. And when he loved me, it felt warm to my spirit. He went out of his way to keep from hurting me; caring son, loving father and respectful, too. It was like a dream to feel so good about feeling so good—no shame, no guilt, no pain, just Saturday morning cartoons, smiles as big as one could hope for and Anita Baker songs on repeat – "Caught up in the rapture of love." Hmmm. He was trustworthy and reliable, and did I mention ambitious? We both were!

Like the 90s cartoon, "Pinky and the Brain," we woke up every day with plans to take over the world. Hard work was no stranger. Time was no object. Nothing was unattainable. I worked weekdays, he worked weeknights. I was working on my doctorate, he spent all day Saturday and half of Sunday taking classes for his Master's degree. We would co-parent his son every other weekend. We were both very close to our families, so that took time and energy. We each had big dreams, so more time and energy. It was a lot. We knew that building an intimate, long-standing bond would be no piece of cake; but we were determined to make it work. The first year was full of surprise dinner visits that turned to bagel runs in the morning. Ninety-minute phone conversations, family outings and shared evenings with friends occupied most of our free time. Both of us acutely aware of the demands of a healthy relationship by this point of our lives, we made sure, despite the difficulty, to create space for truth, communication, expectations, compromise, realism and kindness. He didn't need saving. I didn't need validation. This time romance looked different. Our lives and our love were full of hard work, good times and late-night peanut butter and jelly sandwiches. And we, as ambitious as we both were, couldn't have hoped for more.

Then, a year in, Mr. Cinnamon Smile proposes marriage. Married? Me? After the past years' heartaches, I was convinced that marriage and children were for desperate women who needed that cliché to feel fulfilled. Although Mr. Cinnamon smile and I wanted a future together, I foresaw no legally sanctioned union, children or even pets as part of the equation. I didn't need those social institutions to mark my success. I was now independent and progressive. I fancied myself strong and liberal and happy that way. And I would have stuck to that story too, were it not for that damn smile that melted down every iced nerve in my heart; that made me question my principles and believe in unicorns again. Ahh that smile - it reminded me why I was mesmerized by Disney story endings before I understood their politics.... That damn cinnamon smile!

I guess I could have said no to the proposal, but who says no to the man of their dreams? He had rejuvenated my faith and reinvigorated my courage. I thought, "If any two people can make this work, it's us." If there was a relationship worth working on, or a man worth working with, it was here... in this moment. After all, a year had passed, and we had barely even argued. Any small conflicts were solved within minutes and sealed with kisses. Our most stressful moments involved planning for the future: careers, events, ambitions; and while the details were unclear, the one thing that seemed blessedly secure is that we would enjoy that future, whatever it looked like, together.

Twenty-four months into the romance, in front of 100 of our closest family and friends, we lost ourselves in each other's eyes and promised to love one another forever, to be married forever. The night was a magical one, sun down on the evening of the summer solstice... Outdoors overlooking the water, flowers framing every scene, the smell of lavender carried by the breeze through the trees and into the ocean we overlooked. Perfect weather, only joy rained down that day.

We put off the honeymoon and bought our first apartment together; a co-op in Westchester, which we decorated to our mutual tastes. Everything went so smoothly, like love is supposed to. It was my first time (outside of college) living outside of my family home and nothing could feel safer than having walked out on that limb with him. Our schedules were difficult, but we made it work. We would squeeze in a hug, write a note, steal a kiss. Invitations from other people were refused; ventures that would pull us away from one another declined. We both went the extra mile to maximize our time together. And though exhausted by the work, we seemed bonded by the experience. We hosted Super Bowl parties and high tea. I embraced the role of wife and stepmom. He embraced the role of husband and protector. It was great.

But little by little the things that seemed so easy started to feel so hard. Me waiting up to see that smile, him rushing home to feel my touch, sacrificing a sport or gathering to watch a movie together, it was tiring. Accommodating our schedule differences had grown stale. We didn't want to be flexible, we wanted to be coddled. And what allowances we once made happily, now felt burdensome. I could see the resentment creeping in. I saw his patience starting to thin. Mine too. It was as if our understanding had an expiration date that we had just not seen, and in the midst of us running around, its content had grown sour. Soon, loneliness had returned, ready to claim its place. My most faithful companion, now back again to remind me of why it never fully flees: infatuation fades and leaves a void that needs filling.

I believe he was having the same epiphany. Mr. Cinnamon smile had been married once before and I think that he felt much more comfortable with loneliness, had come to trust it even, as a more reliable reality. For me, loneliness was much harder to re-accept. This time there was no pain of betrayal, no anxiety to cloud the barrenness, no tears; only the ache of disconnectedness as I sat alone in silence, perpetually absent of a man too "good" to begrudge, in a situation too empty to be fulfilling.

It was hard. We missed each other on most days, me running in as he was preparing to run out. Time passed slowly. Fantasies consumed my mind's space. I learned every crevice of every crack on the ceiling of that one-bedroom apartment as I toured each room with loneliness leading the way. Narrating the scene, it reminded me that I was still not good enough for someone to want to be with all the time. Every insecurity seemed magnified by the empty space. Every thought was deafening in the silence; every fear, every desire unimportant with no one to share it with… Until he came home, too exhausted to listen, too in love to ignore me, but too disconnected to care. Little by little the distance between us grew larger, more expansive. It turned us against one another. Soon loneliness had moved into my home and, well, everyone knows that three is a crowd. With it driving a wedge between him and me, rebuilding on our bond became much harder to do.

That loneliness was a tricky adversary, the way that it would run and tell him one thing and then me something different. The space between him and me just got bigger and bigger. And with so much room available, loneliness invited in some of its best friends. The first guest to arrive was desperation. She slept with me, teaching me how to cling, to appear insatiable, assuring me it was safe to yearn, encouraging me to beg. Then came pride. He resided with my husband, shared his side of the bed, taught him to appear unwavering, begged of him to remember that they could live without me, kept him standing his ground. I pleaded with him to spend more time with me, to do more work on our relationship, to quiet the distractions and take a leap of faith with me. Even in his free time, he had started to pick up new hobbies and sports activities. I predicted, fretfully, that if he couldn't put in more time, our connection would start to dissolve. He thought me inconsiderate and impatient, claimed that I "always needed more," heard my prediction as an ultimatum, argued that this was the best he could do for now, and that "more" would be available down the road if I was willing to wait and see it through. I so frantically wanted to, but my desperation was all-consuming. I was so lonely and trying so hard to make him see and make him care. And his pride was so strong, keeping him protected and sheltered from what was real to me. They did quite a job on our egos, those two: pride and desperation. And just when we thought their shifts were over, in to relieve them came resentment and fear.

This time, they alternated between us. I came to feel bitter about pretty much anything that got his attention because I so deeply craved it. He started to resent "having" to spend more time with me because he barely had any time for himself. I started to fear that we were slipping away from one another. He started to fear that this relationship was going to take more than he had to give. Everything started to feel difficult. Hell, impossible. And in that whirlwind of complications came anxiety and pain to live with loneliness once again.

Looking for a way to restore myself, I took a trip to Scottsdale, Arizona, for the intensive component that my Life Coaching certification process required. At this point, I had transitioned into a career in social service, first working as a mediator and then a counselor. The helping professions had caught my eye, but I wasn't into pathology and diagnosis. Plus, being a sociologist who had fallen in love with new age spirituality, I was looking for something interdisciplinary. Life Coaching was a win. He thought it was flighty and a bit esoteric. It wasn't as "respected" or concrete as the fields of interest that he valued. But I was discovering new pieces of me through the readings of coaches like Martha Beck and Iyanla Vanzant and purpose was finally re-entering my vision. I had to do this. I had to go.

In my mind, the trip couldn't have come along at a better time. I figured it would give each of us some space to clear our heads, to miss each other a bit, and to do some of the hard work on ourselves rather than continuing to blame the other. Oh, how we see only what we want to. When I got back home, he had already checked out. It turned out that, with the level of intimacy and abandonment fears that he kept pent up inside, leaving at a time when our relationship was that fragile was one of the most dangerous things that I could have chosen to do. It flagged every trigger for him, called to war all of his defenses. In short, I incited full-on emotional recoil. His vulnerability stepped back as an army of psychological soldiers set up barricades around his heart – the ultimate game of chess and I had lost.

The week I returned, Mr. Cinnamon smile spent most nights at his sister's place. He claimed that she had been his childcare in my absence and he wasn't just going to up and leave her now. Yeah, whatever. We both knew what this was. A few days later, he finally told me that he didn't think he could do this anymore. But I had just had a breakthrough in Scottsdale, in the mist of my loneliness and self-discovery. I didn't want to go from a break-through to a break up. I pushed for us to move away, start fresh, live out the dreams that we had long discussed. That only further overwhelmed him. He believed love should be enough. I required that we work at it. The more that we fought over the destiny of this marriage, the more we finally exposed some of the underlying differences between us. Looking back on it, I realize that our models of what relationships demand and take to survive were completely incompatible. Funny how that never came up while things were going great!

Now, here we were, madly in love and completely exhausted by it—him practically drained, me totally disillusioned. It was a difficult reality to negotiate. At first, I just kept trying to convince him that we could make it work. If only he would reconsider…perhaps we could try prayer, or therapy, or both. It was the closest I had ever come to healthy and happy at the same time, and I was simply not prepared to let it go. The good times were so good and lasted most of our relationship. I wasn't willing to believe that it could just die, seemingly overnight. I had to keep trying. And I did.

For a while it was like we never even had that conversation. I kept cooking as soon as I got home, so that he could eat before he left for work and take food with him. He kept up all the phone calls with updates on what time I could expect him and what was going on at work or with his family. We continued to make love. It almost seemed surreal that we were even breaking up. But as anyone who has been through a breakup knows, the phase of ignoring what is happening can only last for so long. Soon reality reared its ugly head in small things like how to RSVP for an event, what to do about that vacation we were planning or whether I had the right to ask questions about the woman's voice on the other side of that phone call. Just like that, our wounds reopened.

We tried therapy, but he was still so hurt and so afraid. And I was still so impatient and so self-righteous. He wanted the therapist to get me off his back. I wanted the therapist to validate all my feelings and show him how he was wrong. Neither one of us was ready to take responsibility for dismantling what was, unquestionably, the better part of each of our lives. He was mean and cold and did everything in his power to help me hate him, in the hopes that I would let go. I was short-sighted, only able to see all the work that he refused to put in, unable to really value what we had, still requiring more. He was so hurtful. I was so needy. He was so distant. I was so demanding. We were so disconnected.

Still, even after that went wrong, we continued living together. We knew it couldn't work. What we didn't know was how to walk away. I continued to beg him to rethink his position. I've never seen anyone so resolute about anything in my life. It was as if reconsideration could make him vulnerable again and that was a chance that he just didn't seem willing to take anymore. And I would step outside of my body and tell myself to suck it up, pack up my things and leave. But I just couldn't bring myself to actually do it. I felt so strongly against giving up on something that had been 99% perfect. I couldn't let that 1% come to define us. Even after I knew it had.

One morning, in the early Fall of 2007, it all came to a head. He flat out said that there was absolutely nothing that I could ever do to change his mind. Our marriage was over and that I just had to accept it. It's funny; it hurts more to write it now, than it did to hear it then. When he said it, it felt more like an epiphany than a blow; more like relief than rejection. "Fine, he's done, so am I," I thought spitefully. I know now that my defenses had finally kicked in and it was my ego that came to the rescue in that conversation, not acceptance. But back then, what I truly thought was, "Fuck him!" I was no longer willing to continue to put myself out there while he played it safe; to set myself up to be rejected by him time and again in the hopes that he would change his mind. I had been doing that for months. He wanted me to let go, so I let go, with both hands.

With him making more money than me at the time, I would have to be the one to leave. I couldn't afford to keep the apartment, and he could. So, that's what we decided. I would look for another place to live. In the meantime, with my ego so hurt, my dreams so shattered and my heart so broken, I ran straight toward family, friends, parties and alcohol and quickly found myself entangled in the courting of another man. My husband, by his own admittance, had just woken up one morning and decided that he had stopped wanting me as his wife; just like that. And that rejection, humiliation, disappointment, emotional abandonment and loneliness had taken a toll.

I found it hard to resist someone who was so interested in giving me all the love I was begging for and being denied. I entertained it; a few phone calls, a few scheduled meetings at a dance club or two. He was charming, and I could really use some charm. Cinnamon smile and I were roommates by this point, but no one in his peer group knew, until one of them saw me and the new guy out one night and called him to inquire. That was the straw that broke the camel's back. He wanted me out and just like that, I found a place, packed myself up and left. My parents, friends and I moved everything I owned and half of what Cinnamon smile and I bought together in one day, into a studio apartment in the Northeast Bronx, downstairs from where my cousin lived. For the first time, ever, I was officially, living on my own.

Then, like clockwork, Mr. Cinnamon smile calls, pleading for another go at our marriage. It was something right out of the movies. I was so angry at him for believing that he could just turn it all back on now after I had tried so hard for so long with no bending on his part. Screw him. I wasn't going back. Plus, I was seeing this new guy and he was nice to me. I know that sounds silly, but I liked "nice." Right now, I really needed "nice." So, I continued my fling with the other man, briefly; partially out of romance, partially out of spite.

There was no denying, though, that my heart still belonged to that Cinnamon smile. So, we gave it another go: I, just as demanding and self-righteous and, now, even angrier, and he, just as distant and disconnected and, now, even less trusting. I could never get over how he gave up on us, despite how remorseful he appeared to be. He could never get over my fling with another man, even though it took place after our relationship had ended. Technicalities didn't matter. Too much damage had been done.

My husband and I separated again in February of 2008, after an additional three months of trying to make it work and divorced sometime later. He got my heart in the settlement, and I married loneliness in a shotgun, rebound ceremony. I just couldn't stop comparing this moment to how my life "was supposed to turn out." I fixated on the emptiness that now polluted my spirit, focusing on all of the questions that consumed my thoughts, like "Why doesn't he love me? Don't

I deserve to be happy? How do I make this pain go away? Will I ever love this way again? What did I do wrong? Why me?"

My thoughts were not only in control, they were destructive. And the most dangerous of them were the ones that theorized on why I was alone and convinced me that being alone was a sign of failure; I wasn't worthy of being loved or capable of loving another. After all, if I was, someone would be here with me right now, loving me and letting me love them in return. Those thoughts sang me to sleep night after night, as if someone had created a symphony strung together from all of my fears. And the nights I cried don't even compare to the nights that I just couldn't make myself cry anymore. Those are the days when loneliness hurts the most, because you just can't imagine a worse person to be stuck with than yourself.

Poetic Reflection: Love Gone Wrong

I could lose myself for days in the haze and emotional maze
of that addiction
Loved ones insisted that it was just a phase that I should try
harder to escape, but every kiss from his lips condemned me
deeper into its contradictions...
Caught in the confines of my false feelings of freedom,
trapped in the promise of his uncertainty, I was the
protagonist cast to play in this romantic tragedy whose most
sacred truths were all based in fiction...
Fantasy... The fallacies on which we based our most trusted
commitments
"I love yous" and "I'll always be theres" whose honest
intentions meant very little in the face of their impossibility
and affliction
Our connection - a constant source of friction
Our vision blurred by tears that joined alcohol in cocktails of
pain
The love addiction fresh in vein
The high – a jolt to spice the plain
A guiding star to navigate the gray terrain
The only thing worth the self-hatred I became
Each of us... a slave in chains
Bolted down to the idea of one day being able to say
"I feel loved in this"; "I could love myself through this";
"There will still be love at the end of this"; as the cost of
chasing this love became more than either of us could afford
to pay
I mean, who were we kidding, anyway?
Neither of us was truly capable of being who the other wanted
to love
With me so lost and him so scarred, any dreams of releasing
doves

Quickly turned to nightmares about the codependency that
had come to exist between the two of us
And soon all things healthy just seemed too tough
Every promise really a bluff
Soft caresses hardening as their touch turned rough
And as insecurities tightened their grip like handcuffs
All we could do was close our eyes and yell in desperation that
we had both finally had enough!

Part II

Me

From
Loneliness
To
Wellness

Through Our
LATINA LENS

The Happy Jamona

Esmeralda Santiago, in When I Was Puerto Rican, writes about the concept of a "jamona." The book's characters define it as a woman who has never been married and is too old to marry now. They regard it as an insult that implies ugliness. Why? Because in Latino culture, the term "jamona" (spinster) is used describe women who grow old alone. The implication is that they are undesirable. For surely, if someone were interested in them, then they would be wed. They certainly would not choose to be alone, nor would they deliberately create a life for themselves that was about being by themselves. It's all about being part of a couple, of a family, of something that validates your worth by showing that others like you too. Because, of course, it's not enough, never enough, for just you to like you. At least this is what we're encouraged to believe.

The irony of it is that most Latinas are strong, independent thinkers who can do anything on our own. But instead of celebrating it, we're often made to feel bad about it because of some looming, antiquated idea of who and what we are supposed to be; and, because of our fear of becoming this cultural symbol of unworthiness. They say, "mejor estar sola que mal acompañada," (better to be alone then in bad company). Well, if so, then why are we taught to fear solitude and to need companionship? Why are we so often encouraged to focus on others over ourselves and to be willing to sacrifice ourselves in the name of preserving our relationships with others?

I understand the importance of being generous with our time and energy, and of doing for others. But self-sacrifice is not a necessary, or necessarily healthy part of relationships. Nor is it a requirement for being Latina. What if it's possible to be happy alone by learning to love yourself first? In fact, for me, learning to be happy alone was necessary for me to ever truly find happiness with another. So, I submit that there's no shame in being "jamona." Just be a happy "jamona" - whether it is short-lived or life-long. In the end, the one who truly needs to love you... is YOU!

Ms. Independent

By the spring of 2008, I had endured exactly a decade of unhealthy, unhappy romantic relationships. I was tapped out. Every cell in my body ached with the sting of disappointment. All I could enjoy was sleep and chicken wing/biscuit meals from Popeyes. The rest of life seemed bland, inconsequential even. Every day: go to work; hold back the tears; come home; work on the doctoral research; cry; stare at the ceiling until I fall asleep; dream of it getting better; have nightmares of it getting worse. Next day: wake up; get dressed; go to work... No one could tell (the way I carried on with life) that my heart was slowly rotting inside. I was a well-groomed, well-styled zombie.

Already working as a mediator, counselor and life coach – I loved helping my clients put their lives back together, only to watch as mine was falling apart. Something magical seemed to happen in my sessions. It was as if I channeled some divinely inspired wisdom meant only for them, not to be accessed by me. For while I was smart and insightful when it came to solving their problems, I was slow and inaccurate at even identifying my own. What a living contradiction?! I could counsel anyone about anything, but in my meetings with myself, late at night in my bed, the only counselor there to console me was loneliness and the discourse lacked greatly in its divinity. I was alone, and it was mockingly loud – disturbing enough to keep me up all night. I mean, here I was, twenty-eight years old, balancing the writing of my dissertation with the trauma of this divorce, and still trying to get settled into a new job; not to mention trying to do it all with a smile on my face and a strut in my stilettos. I was exhausted. Just managing the process of dragging myself out of bed was laborious enough. I imagine that one of the great things about this world is that it doesn't stop spinning just because relationships end, or fears set in. But, oh, how I wished it would.

The sadness had gotten to be so heavy. Weekends - I didn't even want to get out of bed. Suspicious of any joy that the outside world could possibly have to offer me, I cocooned in the warmth of my duvet. Just me and loneliness, eating packs of pumpkin seeds and binge-watching Law & Order SVU marathons. Leaving the apartment seemed useless. Better to stay home alone. It was safe there; lonely, but safe. And the only thing that had now trumped my fear of being alone, was my fear of being hurt. So, I liked safe. I needed safe.

The days passed so quickly. Soon months of functional weeks and depressing weekends rolled by with even loneliness getting bored of the melancholy and drama. "Would it always be this way," I asked myself when I could peek my head up from the shield of my covers. Would I always be sad when alone? Would I always be sad and alone? Don't get me wrong. I was dating and there were plenty of men around, but few made it to a second date. Fewer even, got in my head. Still fewer made it into my heart and even fewer made it into my bed. Most days and nights, it was just me and loneliness.

The unanswered, desperate questions came by the tons. "What does a sista have to do to get some real love?" At some point, drained and discouraged, I realized that I was once again at the same crossroads that I had visited just four years earlier. Similarly, I had the same choice to make: continue to live, day in and day out, in the anxiety, fear, anger and sadness that was currently eating me alive, or learn how to make it better. Really, those are the only two choices that we ever have: be held hostage by the pain or find a way to recalibrate. We trick ourselves into believing that we can change other people. We pride ourselves in believing that it's really not "us." We con ourselves out of doing the hard work and sell ourselves the dream that with minimal effort on our part we will see a maximum improvement in our lives. But it's all bullshit. We must be the change!

I had to actively entertain the only question that has ever mattered: "What if I'm the problem... and thus, the solution? What if there is something about the way that I think, feel, behave, or live that can actually change the outcomes I experience... if I'm humble enough to consider it, brave enough to attempt it and diligent enough to work at it?" That inner dialogue changed my life. Suddenly, my consciousness started to shift. Not in a way that produced an overnight change in lifestyle, but in a way that got me excited to live again. And that excitement inspired my courage to begin taking responsibility for my own joy; cultivating it and nourishing it.

People say all the time that with great power comes great responsibility. For me the epiphany came in reverse. I realized that with taking great responsibility for my life choices came a great power to affect my life outcomes. No blaming others, making excuses or seeking external change. I had to own my misery if I wanted to create my joy. It was time to start analyzing where my thoughts and actions came from, what they represented for me and what impact they were having on my world. It was time to get to know myself, celebrate what I liked, change what I didn't and connect with the whole of it. **I had spent the last decade falling in and out of love with**

**men who were falling in and out of love with me. It was
time for me to learn how to fall in love with myself.**

So, in 2009, with almost three decades of emotional
baggage neatly stored away in the cabinets, closets and
drawers of my NYC studio apartment, I began a new stage in
my life; one that transformed every part of me, touched my
most inner fabric and took root. I began to heal. The very
definition of which is to restore harmony; to make something
healthy and well again – and wellness was exactly what I was
seeking.

I may not have known it then, but my path to health and
wellness, which seemed so drawn out, chaotic, unpredictable
and personal, in fact mirrored a wellness model that
academics have long proven to be effective in helping people
heal (Swarbrick, 2006). You'll come across many models of
wellness should you choose to do the research, but this is
perhaps my favorite. It's the most comprehensive, in my
opinion, and the one that most perfectly captures the work I
did to heal myself and truly begin to love myself. It pushes
you to seek wellness in eight different dimensions or aspects
of yourself: intellectual, emotional, spiritual, occupational,
financial, social, physical and environmental. It asks you to do
the work necessary in each to honor your greatness, restore
your balance and heal. I discovered it after finding my peace.
Yet, I use it here as an organizing principle for my stories of
healing for it was in those stories that I began to walk my path
to wellness, change my habits and lifestyle, and fall in love
with myself in every dimension of my being!

1.

Expand Your Mind

Suggestions:
Draw,
Write &
Read

Reading was never my favorite activity. In fact, after the gruel of my graduate coursework, I had grown to hate reading. I was slow at it. My mind would wander. I had to read each sentence twice just to have it make sense. It was tough for me to finish any book that I started let alone remember what I read afterward. I certainly was not accustomed to just picking up a book for fun, when I found myself bored or alone like the protagonist of some sophisticated film. I much preferred crime dramas and a reality television show or two (or ten). So, when my cousin suggested some books that she thought might help, I was hesitant. She had gifted me *Conversations with God* (Walsch, 1996) some fifteen years prior and as eye-opening and earth shattering as that was, it had still taken me months to get through it. With life feeling so dull already, I wasn't really in the mood to do something else that I didn't enjoy. I put her latest gift, *Eat, Pray, Love* (Gilbert, 2007) on the book shelf and promised to get to it later.

Instead, I decided to sketch. An "introduction to art" class that I attended during undergrad had sparked an interest in one day further developing a hobby that I enjoyed since childhood: drawing. I found it particularly fun to doodle in charcoal but hadn't done so in a while. This seemed like as good a time as any to pick it back up. Why not use my time alone to do something that I liked? Why not do something creative and expressive; something productive? Why not have something to show for all this time spent by myself? So, I drew. And, oh, how thankful I am that I did.

There is truly something special about the feeling of charcoal being gripped by your thumb, pointer and middle finger that makes you feel like your body is extending right out onto the canvas; or in my case, the small sketchpad that I bought at Barnes & Noble. You should try it some time. It is as if the charcoal becomes a conduit whose sole purpose it is to channel picturesque epiphanies right from your soul, through your fingertips and into the strong lines and soft curves of a newly created image. This image, which did not exist before you, which could not exist without you, is now, somehow a little time capsule containing all the pain that it hurts to hold on to and all the hope that you can't seem to let go of. Each scribble on the page, no matter how simple or profound, serves as a snapshot of your mood, a still of your thoughts' movements - a memory or fantasy or memory of a fantasy that just gets frozen in time. It's magical.

The hours would pass with me sitting, yogi style, on the area rug that I had placed over the cold garage basement floor of that studio apartment. I would ignite the fake flames of my very cute walnut wood fireplace, put on some Streisand, Pac or La India and just sketch. Not because I fancied myself an artist, but because in this loneliness, I needed to chronicle my existence – my experience. I needed to capture its highs and lows. I needed to think. And as I sat to think, I would set my hand free to wander every crevice of the page, leaving charcoal trails of its journey across the ridges of the paper.

I thought of people and places, things I enjoyed and dark moments I suffered. I obsessed over the love that I craved, the pain that I had come to sinfully enjoy and the baggage that I so gravely needed to discard. And I drew – clouds that cried and mermaids that flew, squiggles and circles and abstracts by the dozens. My songs of sadness, pride, lament, fear and excitement, all arranged to the melody of my wrist as I swayed my hand in and out of my mind. It was fun. More importantly it seemed to empty my chest of those heavy breaths; the ones that followed those thoughts that stole my air – those unanswered desperate questions. It was freeing and cathartic.

But at some point, it would end. I would finish a piece, sit back and glance at it and wonder what it meant. Then I would flip through the many pages of pieces and wonder what it all meant: the drawings, the heart ache, this life. Soon my desperate mental conversations would resume loudly and angrily, almost in resentment of having been quieted by the sketching. I was going mad. My left hand throwing the sketchpad in the direction of the fireplace, while my right hand dug its nails into the charcoal, burying it into the dark brown crevices of the rug. I'd curl up into fetal position against the sofa until the slip cover fell over me and cry. Drawing was a temporary ease of mind, but I needed to somehow exorcise my head of the actual words that were haunting me. The "goodbyes" of "ghosts of lovers past," the rejection of dream jobs, the insidious little lies about my inferiority that crept up when I tried to plan a future of joy. Those verbal attacks crashed against my peace like the high waves of the Pipeline on Oahu's north shores. I needed to get them out of my mind. I needed to externalize the struggle.

So, as I had done so many times, so many years before, I looked to poetry for some relief. At first, it came out in a rant of rage. I still had so much anger, so much noise in my soul. It was hard to form coherent phrases. All I could muster were simple words to illustrate my despair: "Scared," "broken," "uninspired," penciled to the page of an old journal. I filled books with collages of uninteresting adjectives, with no verbs to give them life. No movement for them. No movement for me. Just a documenting of the misery. I wasn't much into

71

verbs those days, given how tired I felt. There was no movement to explain. My whole story had become a collection of vague and depressing descriptors. I asked myself, where were the action words? Where was the action? What could I do to change how I felt? What had I done to get here? And little by little, as I explored what had transpired and thought through what I wanted, stories began to fill my head and poems began to fill the page. The first few were free verse memories of times that had past. The next few were revelations of the joy to come. And some of them captured the intensity of what I felt most in the moment.

What I felt, was confused. So, I wrote about it - what I thought it would take to make me happy, what I believed it would look like, what was holding me back. Some rhymed, some did not. Some were image rich, others were tirades. I gave some of them an urban hip hop flare and let others read like the sonnets of Frost. Still, in their diversity they shared one truth. All of them were the chanting of my spirit as it worked its way through the mess that I felt like I had made.

First, I drafted *Have You Seen Me*.

> You think you see me?
> What's fascinating is that you actually think
> that you can see me,
> Hiding behind these shallow walls, drowning
> in my insecurities…

Those were the first lines of the first poem I wrote during this time. It ended in:

> It's all disguised by the masks I've created out
> of fear,
> So, I want to know how you could possibly
> claim to see me, to know me…
> When the truth is that I, myself, haven't even
> seen me in years!

It was the most honest I had been with myself in so long. My truest essence was drowning in a pool of institutions: marriage, graduate school, a career in executive management. I really *hadn't* seen myself, my soul, in years. After I wrote that, the floodgates just opened. Poetic inspiration rained down on me with one beautifully articulated self-criticism after the other. It was painful.

> I never felt like enough…
> To be at peace, to reach happiness, to deserve love
> Instead it was chilly inside and life always felt more like a compromise
> To avoid the lonely nights of cries that would surely come to characterize
> My life if I didn't transform into whoever they thought I was.

That was taken from my *Homage to Loneliness*. We had been partners for so long, loneliness and I. Surely, it deserved a serenade of its own, no? After all, we were clearly in the process of breaking up now and every break up needs a good ballad. It was one of the harder poems to write, because it made the break up real. But, real is exactly what our parting had to be this time. So, I wrote it. And I wrote some more; emotional vomiting, the equivalent of that famous scene from poltergeist. I was in trouble and it was all over the margins of my notepad and the notes app on my smartphone. There was a lot of questioning of faith:

> No one can seem to give me a reason for why I should continue believing in this 'God'
> I hear so much about
> Why they've given Him so much clout, and just let Him run amok

Or how they know that it's Him when things
happen and not just science, fate or luck
And I don't know how to reconcile the fact
that my mind doesn't buy a damn line of the
stories they use to justify His worship
With the chill that I now feel deep down
inside, every time I start to cry and ask for
His mercy
I know that there's something bigger than me
I just don't know what... I'm stuck
And sometimes I just wanna give up!

Most importantly, there was great acknowledgment that I was
ready to heal and just didn't know how:

God, I want to learn to heal; I want to learn
how to trust what I feel
How to design a personality that's much
more on an even-keel
How to summon a self-love that right now
seems so surreal when I hear it described
I want there to be, within me, a gentle tide
So that I might rise to the challenge of
lessening my pride,
Quieting my ego and letting love back inside.

What was pouring out was the humble rumblings of a heart that
had lost its way. And I had no direction with which to guide it.
Sketching was a rejuvenating distraction. Poetry was a cathartic
release. But the sadness brewing inside was replenishing itself
at a rate more rapid than what I could expel. I needed to do
more than to just let it out. I needed to learn how to stop it
from coming back.

In a state of severe desperation, I sought out the advice of
people who had found a way to create happiness from chaos:

gurus, teachers, anyone who had a story to tell that could help move my story toward a more positive trajectory. And those stories were most easily found in their books. So, despite my difficulty with reading, it was time to buckle down. I wasn't really in a position to cling to my limitations. It was time to suck it up and see what I could learn from the many thought leaders whose works my cousin had recommended; people who had figured much of this "happiness work" out.

I reached for *Eat, Pray, Love* first. It was the newest addition to my library and the plot which most closely resembled my current situation: recently divorced writer on a search for self. I was skeptical at first given all the hype around the book. That is, until I started getting into it. Then I was immediately moved by Gilbert's triumph in the face of similar struggles. I connected with her. She too, had met loneliness along her travels. She had also made peace and found love and that excited me. I liked her writing. I liked her story. But what I liked most was how I felt when I finished her book; invigorated. My mind had expanded. New ideas had been introduced. I had suggestions to experiment with and lessons to apply. Perhaps reading wasn't so bad after all.

So, I re-read *Conversations with God* – all of them. In fact, I re-read several books that helped me grow throughout my early 20s, including *A Return to Love* (Williamson, 1992), *The Power of Intention* (Dyer, 2005) and *Finding Your Own North Star* (Beck, 2001). Then I acquired a few more books of a similar nature: the works of Millman (2006) and Hay (2004). Then another Gilbert book, this time *Committed* (2011). Over the coming years, I took a specific interest in the memoirs of women: Assata Shakur (2001), Cheryl Sandberg (2013), Sonia Sotomayor (2014), Immaculée Ilibagiza (2006), Malala Yousafzai (2015). Everywhere I turned, there were happy and successful people who had battled their own demons on the path to inner peace and outer progress. What the fuck was I crying about? They motivated me to embrace my resilience; to live my purpose. Their stories touched me.

I read until I couldn't read anymore and then I took a nap. When I woke up, I read again. Despite how hard it still was and how many episodes of "Real Housewives" I had on my DVR, I read. I highlighted and underlined and tabbed pages. I paid close attention and absorbed everything I could. And I became a reader - one who seeks out insight in the perspectives of others – one who reads to learn. I do now think of myself as a life-long learner, considering how little I find I know given the grandness of this universe.

So now, I read to learn. In fact, I've read more in the past eight years, than in the 28 that preceded them. I guess you can say that I'm a newly converted enthusiast of reading, because of the way it helped my brain to stretch itself and my thoughts to transform. The written word is just so powerful. In my solitude, it allowed me to be surrounded by masters, mentors and teachers who had experienced pain, discovered truths and found ways to be fulfilled. And what I learned from them so profoundly transmogrified my spirit, that suddenly poetry and sketching also became purely joyous again. The sting they once brought had now faded and in my time alone, I could read, sketch and write and feel nothing but happily alive.

~ Research & Wrap-Up ~

Take some time to try drawing your feelings. We have good reason to believe that it can be helpful. In fact, Slayton, D'Archer and Kaplan (2010) conducted a study that concluded the following:

> A variety of mental health, developmental, and medical patient groups are represented in our review and many include behavior problem profiles. We now have some evidence that art therapy can lead to positive treatment outcomes for these populations. (p.116)

You may also want to try your hand at writing what you feel. Stuckey and Nobel (2010) stated:

> Studies have shown that, relative to control group participants, individuals who have written about their own traumatic experiences exhibit statistically significant improvements in various measures of physical health, reductions in visits to physicians, and better immune system functioning. Writing increases health and wellness… (p.259)

While you're at it, think about increasing how much you read and look for some helpful material. According to Pehrsson and McMillen (2007):

> Bibliotherapy is effective in promoting problem solving, increasing compassion, developing empathetic understanding and enhancing self-awareness. (p.1)

So, try drawing, writing and reading as ways to expand your mind and improve your intellectual wellness.

2.

Find Your Center

Suggestions:
Practice Meditation,
Self-Change &
Healthy Love

What I learned from the stories and guidance of those whose works I read was the discipline to control my feelings, instead of letting my feelings control me. It was a tough lesson; one upon which I still find myself constantly building. But these days the work is so much more beautiful and light. I can breathe right through any internal discord and gather my faith with enough time to move easily through the world. Not like back then. Back then, everything was so strenuous: working, relaxing, it was all so difficult. I knew that I had to get my feelings in check, but how?

The most consistent advice I found on this was to learn to meditate – to observe the activity of my mind as would an outsider and hush it to rest. And trust me, with a mind as busy as mine, shutting it down would prove to be no easy task. I had to learn to really listen to what was going on inside if I was serious about learning to quiet it. So, I turned off the television, put my smartphone on "Do Not Disturb" and sat. No distractions, no external noise, no paper, no pen, no charcoal; just me and the incessant stream of consciousness that rented space in my head. How scary it is to be alone with your thoughts, no? After all, that's the hardest part of being alone. That you finally must just shut up and listen... to yourself. The loudness of your disappointments, the screeches of your regrets, the screams of your good-byes; anger, hope, judgment, love, and fear all waiting to be played out like voicemails that have been accumulating in your inbox for years.

It was hard. I would sit, again, in yogi pose: this time on the edge of my bed. Hours would pass with me trying to silence my thoughts; keyword - "trying." Instead, I would ruminate on how I got here and what the next step should be. I felt paralyzed by my past. I was perpetually obsessed with my future and I was even more, undeniably, uncomfortable with anything that characterized the present moment. It was so scary. So many stories and sagas playing out in there. I had become accustomed to them just being background noise to whatever I had going on at any given moment. But now they were the stars of the show.

The conflicts, the many contemplations, pieces of my mind that just rant all the time, without my conscious awareness – were front and center – and sloppy. There was absolutely no method to their madness. I was surprised to see that much of what my mind fixated on was arbitrary. Any "legitimate" worries were about things over which I simply had no control. The insecurities that popped up were based on one or two perceived failures that could be easily outweighed by my successes, should I have chosen to give those some airplay. The fears I heard in my ears came from unreliable sources. It was a wreck!

It was an ocean of madness above a deep floor of debris, with sunken pirate ships and deadly stingrays. And I now had the pleasure of diving into it, on a hunt to rescue the many treasure chests and magical aquatic creatures drowning and burning in my sea of thoughts. Great! What a rescue mission to be sent on, especially since I'm the one who sank the ships to begin with. I wondered how I could be trusted to save a serenity that I had ruined in the first place. And yet, that was my charge. So, I accepted it. If I was serious about making peace with myself, it was time to take this plunge. I dove in with about an hour of oxygen and no way to communicate with the outside world. Funny how I'm not even that good of a swimmer and here I was, about to go deep-sea diving.

"Okay Dinorah, this is going to be very overwhelming. Let's start. Just listen to these thoughts without believing them, dwelling on them or acting on them," I would tell myself. "They won't hurt you if you don't engage them. Just watch them swim by like vegetarian Great Whites. Stay focused on the treasure chests. That's where your truth lies." I would shut my eyes and with closed lids focus on the open space right between them. "There's the treasure chest Dinorah. Swim toward it." Then a million thoughts would pop into my head – what I dreamt of last night, that bill I forgot to pay, what I could be doing with this time, what I shouldn't have said at dinner last night.

"They're just vegetarian Great Whites Dinorah, focus on the treasure chest." I tried. But here came more random thoughts of what I would eat for dinner, how I hate to cook, would that affect my relationships, would I ever have a relationship again and suddenly I was being devoured by what were supposed to be vegetarian Great White sharks. To say that it was hard to keep my mind silent is an understatement. Eventually I'd tire and a flicker in the lights would suddenly make my eyelids pop open. If I got one second of quiet mind for that whole hour of "meditation," it was a miracle.

It was so discouraging. I had no control over what was going on in there. It felt like I never would. But the more I practiced, the better that "1 second:1 hour" ratio got. Soon I got two seconds of quiet mind out of the hour. Then three. Before I knew it, I could shut my brain down for a minute or so at a time. There were still sharks, but they vanished out of my focus quicker and quicker. The water was murky, but as long as I concentrated on getting to that chest, I could keep the path ahead of me clear. "Don't get distracted by the seaweed and floating pieces of the wreckage, Dinorah. Focus." And focus is exactly what I did. The more times I meditated, the further I got. Until, I eventually reached the chest. I knew I was doing something right when I opened it and inside was yet another ocean. "Screw it," I thought. "Time to jump in again."

I gained a great deal from the practice of meditation. Not only did it help me develop the discipline to stop the momentum of unhealthy thoughts, it helped me to supplant them with more joyous ones. And by helping me to take control of my thoughts, I also gained control over my feelings. I really began to understand them as my own – as generated by my psyche, informed by my experiences and under my control. They were not the fault or duty of anyone but me. Others were not any more responsible for my emotions than I was for theirs. We each had to take responsibility for what/how we chose to feel. What an astounding revelation to come to after a decade of stormy relationships.

I contemplated the many years I spent arguing, crying, pleading, screaming, reasoning and praying for "him" to change. So many internal resources expended trying to define the experiences and journeys of my lovers. To what end? To make me feel better? To make me happier? Why had I not chosen to focus on my own change, instead? So much of my energy and time used to convince my romantic partners that they should change, all the while my own choices were going unchallenged, many of which were keeping me stuck in unhealthy romances. Instead I focused on the other person. I fell in love with who I thought these men could be, and how happy I thought they could make me, if they just worked at it hard enough.

The problem was that the entire time that I spent in love with their potential, I was actually in relationships with their present choices. And there was the tragic discrepancy. They weren't who I wanted them to be. They were who they were, and they had shown themselves to me from the start. Yet, I felt resentful and angry that I was getting cheated out of having the happiness that I deserved just because the man that I wanted wasn't ready or capable of being the man that I needed him to be. Crazy? Here I was, painting myself the victim of these romantic tragedies when in reality, the dishonest one was me – making believe that I loved them when the entire time what I loved was: (1) The idea of who I thought they could be (2) How valuable it would make me feel to think that I helped them get there, and (3) The fact that trying to change them was a welcomed distraction from having to work on me. The first was a naïve illusion; the second, an egotistical delusion and the third, well that was just plain old lazy fear.

I was placing my happiness in the hands of men with whom I felt a connection. Then, I was killing myself trying to change them into what I thought a worthy "happiness holder" would look like. And I thought the problem was that they wouldn't change? "No Dinorah, the problem was that you gave them your damn happiness to hold. HE-LLO!" It was time to wake up out of this state of perpetual codependency and change myself into the kind of woman that could hold her own happiness. So, that is what I did. I made a commitment sometime around 2010, to be responsible for my own joy. It was on me to own my emotions; to figure out what made me smile and to do it; to figure out what hurt my heart and refuse it. I chose to follow my own journey toward self-growth, with or without a partner, and let the chips fall where they might. No more trying to change "him." He either is what I want, or he isn't.

They say that people don't change, but that's not true. People do change. You're doing it right now, as you read through this book and become inspired to make different choices. What I learned, however, is that people only make lasting change when it is of their own free will, at their own pace and in their own time. The more I reflected on my past, the clearer that it became: to believe that I can facilitate change in people is hopeful. It's why I wrote this book. It's why I do much of what I do. But to insist or demand that people change so that they fit into my scheme of how the world should be, is unjust and ineffective. Ultimately, change is a choice that one makes for him/herself. People do not change until they are ready to. So, I can introduce people to differences and expose them to other ways, the way that so many people do for me. But, if I want more out life, I must <u>be</u> more! Because the only person that I can/should change is me.

Instead of obsessing over changing others, I focused on who I wanted to be. I challenged myself to imagine the best version of me and to become that. And I made a conscious decision to remain alone and to stay out of a relationship unless I was that better person and so was he; no change required. Because then, and only then, could his love feel good to my truest soul and my love feel good to his.

A decade spent in and out of love, consumed by how special it made me feel to be loved. And now, after so much heartache, I had finally learned one very vital certainty: "if" someone loves me is far less important than "how" someone loves me. What an epiphany. Oh, how swept up I had gotten in the "I love him," "He loves me" part of my relationships. It had become the justification to hold on beyond reason, to invest beyond reward, to keep trying to "make things work." All the while I never bothered to ask, "So what if he loves me... do I like how it feels?" See, what the many "I love yous" had failed to capture is *how* he would love me and how I was likely to be left feeling by that love. That's the information that I really needed.

I wish Mr. Caramel Eyes would have said, "I love you, but let me warn you that because of my childhood trauma and my current living situation, that love is going to feel more like pain, nine times out of ten." That would have been very helpful. But, obviously, it would have ruined the mood. It's so much dreamier to leave it at "I love you." So, he did. And apparently, that was all I needed. I stop now and wonder how unlovable I must have thought myself to be, to be so impressed by the mere fact that these men "loved" me; with no real discretion around how it was making me feel. It was sad, really. But now, that I had spent some time learning to love myself more, and better, I was to be far less moved with a man loving me. All that would matter now was how it felt when he did.

I now understood that while love is important, it's not the only component of a healthy and happy relationship. Healthy relationships are built on trust, respect, honesty, shared values and admiration. They take hard work, but they make it feel easy. They're open to the natural evolution of our souls; not resistant to our growth. Most importantly, they are not painful. Instead, they are enjoyable and rejuvenating.

So, when I did start dating again, if the love or even the "like" was more harmful than helpful or was simply not healthy in how it made me feel, I just loved myself well enough to let go… and walk away! Not angrily. Just in recognition of the fact that I want and deserve a love that consistently inspires joy. And so, does the other person and if this isn't it, then why be unhappy? There was a time when I needed things to get really bad for me to leave. Now, I need things to be really great, if I am to stay. I stand firm in my setting of high expectations - No explanations, no wavering!

~ **Research & Wrap-Up** ~

Why not try meditation? Many studies, such as that of Davis and Hayes (2011), confirm its benefits:

> ...research indicates that meditation may elicit positive emotions, minimize negative affect and rumination, and enable effective emotion regulation. (p.200)

It will assist you in engaging in self-awareness and self-change. As Morin (2011) helps us understand:

> Self-awareness is beneficial (the why question) mostly because it makes self-regulation and inference about others' mental states possible. (p.818)

We know that level of awareness also to be helpful in creating and sustaining happy relationships. Healthy love, however, requires us to be diligent in other areas of our lives as well. In fact, Olson, Olson, and Larson (2012) found that:

> The five areas most predictive of happy versus unhappy couples were (in rank order): communication, flexibility, closeness, personality compatibility, and conflict resolution. Happy couples had significantly higher scores (positive couple agreement) on these five areas compared to unhappy couples. (p.4)

So, try engaging in meditation, self-change and healthy love as ways to find your center and improve your emotional wellness.

3.

Soothe Your Soul

Suggestions:
Be Humble,
Grateful &
Faith-Full

People often speak of firm personalities with such condemnation. Particularly, in the case of women, being firm gets you quite a reputation. Try to set an expectation of greatness, with no wiggle-room and no apology. Listen for all the names you will be called: "aggressive," "bitchy," "diva." I was certainly no exception. Having been raised in a family that didn't respond much to meekness, I was not only firm in my expectations, I had also grown to be very sassy, kind of loud and pretty irrepressible – still am. I ran in circles that respected boisterousness and even in my professional life, I found myself needing to be resolute and unwavering. Firmness came quite easy to me, especially now that I was more clear about what I really wanted.

So, as you might imagine, the last of the things on my self-improvement list that I was eager to work on was, "be humbler." All the enlightened masters I read were described this way, so I was sure that I would have to tackle it at some point on my road to enlightenment; but to be honest, every inch of my being rejected the meekness associated with my perception of humility. I had no interest in becoming the woman who gets overlooked, except for when she's walked all over, all in the name of spiritual enlightenment. I wasn't into being docile and demure. "Humble," just wasn't my thing. That is, until one day I walked into a meeting of this character development group that I joined. It was led by a Rabbi who spoke of humility as having a healthy self-esteem, midway between self-abasement and arrogance. The concept of humility, per her teachings, was about taking up an appropriate amount of space in the world, not too much and not too little. It was not about shrinking yourself into nothing, or about aggrandizing yourself into legend. It was about understanding that we are each made of greatness, and yet, so is everything else. I had not heard humility spoken of in such a way until then. It resonated with me.

In its most profound rendition, humility is about the understanding that you deserve no less than greatness and that pursuit of your own greatness is also how you honor the greatness in others. Suddenly, it became clear. For so long I had confused humility with meekness and docility and it had convinced me that being humble and being firm were mutually exclusive qualities. But I came to understand it differently. It is not about being meek, docile or passive. It's about understanding that – I am both nothing and everything all at once. I can bask in my brilliance and, at the same time, recognize how much I have yet to learn. That is the grandness of this universe. The energy and life that fills everything is the same energy that created me. The birds that wake us with song, the grass that grows at our feet, the sun we look to for warmth; they are both simple and extravagant all at once.

I have always found that revelation to be inspiring, but since re-envisioning my idea of humility, I make an even more concerted effort to remember, more consistently, that this marvelous energy that fuels me, also resides in all that surrounds me. It's not just in the glorious waves of the oceans or the colorful flowers that bloom. It's also inside the young cashier that won't get off her cell phone to answer my price check question. It's in the guy who cut me off on the highway this morning. It makes up the snow that I curse at when it starts to fall and the beach that I love to walk on under the warm sun. It's everywhere! It encourages the compliments and criticisms of me that I hear from others. It births my indulgences and my lessons. It takes no prisoners and plays no favorites. It moves mountains and possesses stillness. It's everyone and everything. Thus, to truly be humble, I must delight in my grandeur AND marvel at my insignificance.

Connecting to the greatness around me and to the greatness within me has helped to nurture yet another important spiritual practice: gratitude. Understanding my alignment with this wondrous universe helped me to fall deeper in love with myself. And the more in love with myself that I fell, the more grateful I became for any and every experience that had ever contributed to my growth. After all, to love the sum is to love its pieces. So, to acknowledge the perfection of anything, is to acknowledge the perfection of the many seemingly imperfect circumstances that it took to create that thing as it now is.

If we resulted from the same energy that created our world(s) then it would logically follow that we carry the beauty and power of that energy; a beauty and power that is easy to love. And when you truly love yourself, then it is difficult not to be grateful for the beautiful orchestration of everything that has ever impacted your development. For had any small detail been different, you would not be who you now are.

Every trial and tribulation that I have ever experienced, provided an opportunity for me to feel, to learn and to flourish. Had I not experienced that massive depression in my mid-20s, influenced by unhealthy romance, unsteady faith and unemployment, I would never have been humble enough to agree to the $26k/year position that I took as a Mediator, even after I had a Master's Degree. That position placed me in the school where I later worked as a counselor, which inspired me to pursue a career in life coaching. That career drove major developments in my personal and professional growth, not to mention providing me with the opportunity to connect with, help and learn from so many others. Had my marriage not ended, I may never have lived alone and made peace with the loneliness I had come to so desperately fear. That separation and subsequent divorce ushered in what was inarguably one of the largest emotional and spiritual growth spurts of my life. It gave me the space to reconnect with my interests, to relish in my joys, to discover my passions, to face my fears and to reclaim my sense of self. And from that place of inner-peace, I could manifest the lovely and exciting life that I now live.

The fabric of my being is collaged of colorful satins and dreary scraps and a bunch of other crap that I may not have woven together had I been left to my own devices. But when I stand back to admire it as a whole, I realize that the contrast created by that mix is precisely what enhances its beauty. The juxtaposition of lights and darks, the diversity of textures, the complexity of its varied patterns, they all blend to form the perfect high-fashion quilt of life and personality. It is so clear now – the way that experiences were stitched together so perfectly to get me to this moment. And because I was finally at peace with who and where I was at this moment, I could recognize the wisdom of having lived through those experiences – of having earned each patch.

So now, every day, I stop to recall the many things for which I am grateful. I include all my senses and all my faculties. I refer to all my family, all my friends and all the people with whom I don't particularly get along because I know that they are equally important to my growth and experience. I marvel at nature – the plants, the animals, the stars. I focus on the positive opportunities that have manifested. I call on the great things that are yet to reveal themselves. I lose myself in memories of great times. I commemorate the tough times that made me stronger and I think to myself, "I'm so fortunate." The lists go on for pages when I choose to write them. Other times, I can just rant on and on in my mind for an entire bus ride, or traffic jam.

It is amazing how gratitude has transformed my life. Every second of every day now seems easier when I focus on the positive and actively seek the many things for which to be grateful. Things that I once saw as traumatic, I now see as educational. The sadness that I once felt, I now look back on as ignorance – I couldn't see the gift it brought with it and I didn't know how to get "well" enough to get out of it. All my thoughts seem to coalesce around one theme: I have much for which to be grateful.

I often advise my clients to practice gratitude regularly to help improve their sense of wellness. On occasion, I will be told by someone that they "don't have much for which to be grateful" and I challenge them, the way I once challenged myself. Whatever you look for, you will find. If you look for reasons to feel victimized and slighted, you will find them. If you look for reasons to feel fortunate and grateful, you will find those too. So, take the time to think about all the wonderful things that you do benefit from and focus on them. Practicing gratitude will work wonders for you… It did for me!

Gratitude and humility are both very important to my spiritual wellness. Faith is another key component – one which I must admit wasn't always easy for me. As a child, I struggled with what faith should look like. My father's family was very Roman Catholic: baptism, religious instruction, communion, church on Sundays. My mother's family practiced an Afro-Caribbean religion known as Yoruba: rituals and ceremonies that lasted days at a time, folktales and rites of passage. My dad was pretty convinced that we are the descendants of aliens. My mom was clear that we owed everything, first to God, then to a hierarchy of other deities and then to the spirits of ancestors put here to guide us. With such a diversity of influences, it was no wonder I was constantly searching for some clarity. In middle school, I remember accompanying friends to nondenominational churches, synagogues, and prayer groups. As I got older, I travelled the world to pyramids and temples. Over the years, I sat with scholars, argued with priests, prayed, cursed the heavens and questioned almost everything. And in my journeys (both internal and external) I found few answers and more questions.

For over three decades, I waited for my "come to Jesus" moment: some sort of spiritual awakening to clarify my faith and put an end to my searching. But no one moment surfaced. Instead, what I found was a series of moments that helped me to arrive at the following conclusion: There is an undeniable source of energy that clearly created me and the world in which I live. And in some ways, it is helpful to understand that there is something much larger than me at work here. Something that is omniscient and omnipotent because it is responsible for all that was, all that is and all that will ever be. At the same time, it is also helpful to understand that because I am made of that energy and constantly surrounded by that energy, that greatness is also always accessible to me and therefore must also always be accessible to the world, through me.

What is also undeniably true is that that energy source, which breathed life into me and all that surrounds me, has never left me for I still breathe. It could never leave me while I still breathe and will commune with me after my last breath. And in its connection to me and in its companionship, there is solace. For if it can build mountains and fill oceans, if it can power the sun and guide the winds, if it is strong enough to create and sustain the life force of billions, then it can surely keep an eye out for me.

After some research, it turns out that I, right now, am an agnostic panentheist. This basically means that I don't claim to be 100% sure of anything but I do, deep down somewhere, truly believe in God as a force that penetrates absolutely everything. I wrote "God" in the previous sentence because of my upbringing and orientation, but it could just as easily be replaced with Allah, Olofi, Jehovah, the universe, or any number of other terms we have used to label source energy. For they are all just words in a manmade language, which in and of itself is incapable of fully describing such an intangible force. Frankly, I think it's quite silly the way that we obsess about settling on one or two words or even ideals to capture the massive energy behind all things. We argue over semantics and kill each other over the arrogance that we somehow know every detail of truth about the greatest life force that's ever been. I suppose that has much more to do with satisfying our fear-based human need to put things in clear boxes that will help us to feel more in control. It certainly cannot be about using our words to create an accurate image of what we are attempting to describe here, for no words would suffice. The energy behind all things defies the limitations of our vocabulary and I believe we only limit our connection to it by trying so hard to narrowly define it.

Here's what else I believe: I believe in the tears of joy that fill my heart when I hear Gospel music. I believe in the humility I feel when I marvel at nature. I believe in the relief I feel when things go my way and the hope that shadows the disappointment that I feel when they don't. I believe that many teachers have shown us how to connect to the purity of that source's intention: Jesus, Buddha, the Dalai Lama, Abraham, my seven-year old niece when she speaks in moments of inspiration about the simplicity of life. And I believe that my parents are probably both right too. Aliens and Deities (maybe they are one and the same). Who knows? Who needs to know? Why?

Here's what I do not believe. I do not believe that any one religious doctrine has a monopoly on the connection to source energy. In fact, it is our diversity of ideas, experiences and orientations that enrich the human spirit, and everyone must find what works for them. I do not buy into the idea that any one person or group has figured it all out. And what's more, I stopped believing that "figuring it all out" is even a worthwhile goal.

The truth is that faith is far less about the strength of the philosophical arguments that we use to justify our separation from others and explain away our pain and our purpose. It is much more about learning to trust your connection to a divinity that is often inexplicable, but also undeniable. It's about seeing the human connection to that divine energy, in yourself and in others. It's about honoring that connection, every chance you get.

For, in our ability to rest in the peace of that connection, in the grandness of what we represent there is an acknowledgement of the abundance of energy moving through the world at light speed because we are light. And in that recognition of the divinity we cannot ignore inside and all around - in that unequivocally sacred moment of clarity, we find faith. So, if you're ever having a hard time believing in something so spectacular that it makes you feel spectacular too, simply look around you... look inside you. Philosophy you can debate and religion you can denounce, but the existence of a powerful, divine energy cannot be denied! Call it whatever you want. The details are inconsequential. All that matters is that you call it, because it will answer.

~ Research & Wrap-Up ~

Be humble and do so in ways that balance all you have to offer with all you have to learn. Rowatt et al. (2006) show us that:

> ...there could be several benefits afforded to those who exhibit humility... Chief Executive Officers who possessed a rare combination of extreme humility and strong professional will were catalysts for transforming a good company into a great one. Humility could also open the door to intellectual growth... (p.199)

You might find that another helpful practice for growth and success, is gratitude. Work to be grateful, constantly and consistently. Emmons and Stern (2013) remind us that:

> A number of rigorous, controlled experimental trials have examined the benefits of gratitude. Gratitude has one of the strongest links to mental health and satisfaction with life of any personality trait—more so than even optimism, hope, or compassion. Grateful people experience higher levels of positive emotions such as joy, enthusiasm, love, happiness, and optimism, and gratitude as a discipline protects us from the destructive impulses of envy, resentment, greed, and bitterness. (p.848)

You'll likely also see similar benefits from learning to have faith. Miller-Perrin and Mancuso (2015) found that:

> While the relationship between faith and emotional well-being is complex and likely often bidirectional in nature, there is a research basis from which to conclude that faith is one avenue for nurturing positive emotional qualities. While faith is by no means the only avenue to positive emotions, numerous faith variables are associated with emotional health and well-being, including self-rated importance of religion and spirituality, religious and spiritual well-being, and religious and spiritual beliefs and behaviors. (p.45)

So, try being humble, grateful and faith-full as ways to soothe your soul and improve your spiritual wellness.

4.

Balance Your Career

Suggestions:
Love What You Do,
Do What You Love &
Answer Your Calling

With my faith in the universe stronger than ever, believing in myself became easier and easier. It was now time to start realizing all of those dreams that I had long ago put on hold. All of those professional ambitions that I feared would never manifest. It was time to take a leap - time for my professional life to start reflecting the faith, freedom and fulfillment that had finally begun to fill my personal life. It was time for my workdays to be more joyous and my time filled with less bureaucracy and more opportunities for creativity. This was a moment in time for which I was so ready - ready in my spirit, like I had never quite been ready before. So, I started to ponder how I would modify my life to begin pursuing these dreams.

You see, at this point, I had progressed into executive management in the nonprofit/social service sector. So, between an excess of funding issues, a few challenging and exhausting personalities and the stressful minutia of administration, creativity and joy were just not in abundance. And while I was finally ready for a career shift, I also knew that it could be a while before I could make a living doing what I loved. So, I figured that in the meantime, I would find ways to love what I was already doing.

I focused on the strong sense of satisfaction that I got from the work that I did, because I knew the needs of under-resourced communities and the valuable resources that social service agencies provide them. I also understood, intimately, how easily social services can be ripped from communities that need them if those services are poorly administered. So, I worked hard to manage them well.

I decorated my office with inspirational quotes and positive affirmations, fun warm colors, no clutter, lots of open space. I kept tea on my desk and tried harder and harder to glance away from the computer screen and out the window, past the cars streaming up and down the street and onto the lovely oaks being kissed by sunlight as they danced in the backspace of my view.

I made lists of the things that I loved about the job and focused my attention on the positive aspects of my profession. I tried to reframe hurdles as opportunities and while I was still the first to say that something sucked if I felt that it did, I quickly moved off that point toward the circumstance's strengths and a strategy for solving the problem.

I focused on those parts of the job that I was particularly good at: strategic planning, talent development, coaching, budgeting, research, outcome evaluation, systems and structures - throwing those skills at any problems that came my way. And when I had a moment, I switched my focus to my areas of limitation: using diplomacy to build relationships with key figures, task delegation, taking every challenge so personally, being too opinionated and putting in too many hours - all of this, I worked on improving.

I enrolled in leadership trainings, watched webinars, did a plethora of research on reflective leadership and Zen management and brought practices like yoga and meditation into private moments in my office. Not metaphorically either, I quite literally kept a yoga mat in the corner of my office. Sometimes, during the "lunch hour" which I prided myself in rarely taking, I would unroll it and sit. I mostly did it after having been pissed off by something someone said. On occasion, I would do it when I was pissed off by something that I said. Either way, I took a break to cleanse my mind of thoughts, in meditation or relaxation, before re-engaging the world.

I focused a large body of effort on capacity-building with my staff as well, so they could improve in their areas of limitation and maximize their strengths. Not only did I encourage staff to pursue additional training whenever available, I facilitated many trainings myself and made it a point to sit with employees who were interested: to teach them step-by-step, and pass on skills, tools and techniques that could help them to more effectively and efficiently perform and progress.

I built an emotional boundary that kept me from checking emails and working outside of the office. Sure, I was no stranger to the 60-hour week, but at least I was able to leave work at work. That, coupled with vacations every three months, kept me from burning out, becoming resentful or losing perspective. I usually came back from trips refreshed and more creative than before. If I couldn't afford to leave the country, I trooped it to another state. And if none of that was doable at the moment, a stay-cation kept me centered.

While at work, I spent time with colleagues that I knew that I could trust - not the office gossips, the complainers or the pessimists that seem to plague every office. I joined organizational committees and office groups, which engrossed me in everything from dialectical behavioral therapy to cookie bake exchanges (for which I always purchased cookies, because I don't bake very well). I bonded with strong people whose resilience I admired, whose brains I could pick, who thought creatively about problem solving, who were open to thinking outside of the box and who respected me, in the way that I respected them.

I made sure to speak my mind about things that mattered in a way that, hopefully, other people could hear - not offensively or aggressively, but certainly assertively and firmly enough to be taken seriously. And when it was more appropriate (which was more times than I could have ever anticipated), I shut up... And listened and learned from so many who had so much to teach me.

The entire adventure was an exercise in developing a strong work-life balance, which is pretty hard to do when you work so much that it feels like work becomes your life. It was tough, but it was also fantastic. I gave it all I had and used it for all I could learn. And I was reasonably happy. I was loving what I did, but in my soul, there was still something not quite right. It's as if I was being called by another purpose. This other vision of who I wanted to be and what I wanted to be doing was still etched into my spirit like a prophetic tattoo of some sort. In fact, it felt more like a premonition than a desire - like a preview of what was awaiting me if I could only find the courage to pursue it.

So, I mustered all of the humility, gratitude and faith that I could manage and turned in my letter of resignation. It had now been seven years since I earned my life coaching certification, three years since I completed my PhD and a year and a half since I started playing with the idea of going into business for myself. Fortunately, the entire time, I had been coaching clients on the side, teaching at universities part-time as an adjunct, freelance writing, working on my art, and facilitating trainings and workshops on self-help topics. So, I was going into entrepreneurship with almost a decade of experience in my chosen fields. But because I had also been working full-time throughout those years, trying to climb the executive ladder, I had never quite put my all into any of those endeavors. Now, it was finally time!

In Japanese culture, there exists a concept known as Ikigai. Everyone is believed to have one - a reason for being - it's why we wake up in the morning. It often requires that we search deep inside, but the journey is well worth the level of life satisfaction that is believed to come from finding our Ikigai. In fact, many use the word to mean well-being and purpose, with connotations about joy. It is that sacred of an experience.

The conceptual framework for understanding one's Ikigai is complex and as such, is usually presented in a venn diagram of four overlapping circles that form the semblance of a cross. The top circle represents what you love to do - what tasks and activities bring you joy. The circle placed to the lower left of that encompasses those things at which you are very good - areas where you shine. Where these two overlap, those are your passions. The diagram continues with a bottom circle that sits just under the first, and to the lower right of the second, slightly overlapping with both. This one encompasses those things for which you can be paid - sources of income. Where it overlaps with the second, those things are your profession. Finally, to the upper right of that one, slightly overlapping with the others, is a circle containing those things which the world needs. And where that circle overlaps with the last, we can see your vocation. But where that circle overlaps with the first (those things that you love to do), we find your mission. And at the center of it all, at the vortex of intersecting, overlapping snippets of passion, profession, vocation and mission, is your Ikigai.

I was determined to live my Ikigai, to merge my passions and mission into a professional vocation, and a successful one at that. So, I began to strategize. Then I cried (afraid and overwhelmed at the size of my dreams). Then I meditated. Then I prayed. Then I smiled (soothed by the size of my God and my faith). Then I got to work.

I made a list of jobs that I had in the past - things that I enjoyed doing and areas in which I had some experience that I could leverage: teaching, coaching, training, writing. Then I focused on securing consulting gigs in each of those fields. That allowed me the flexibility to focus on building my brand and to make sure that I still enjoyed doing these things as much as I once remembered. Just like that, I seemed to have filled the top and bottom circles - that which I loved and that for which I could be paid. But what about those side circles. I needed a better sense of what I was good at, and what I could offer the world that it actually and truly needed. I took a few deep breaths and thought. Then, I sat back and observed.

Now that I was ready to pay attention, the universe seemed more ready than ever to respond. Family, friends, colleagues and even perfect strangers began to remind me with their words of what a poor job we do of taking care of ourselves, focusing on our growth, investing in our energy and evolving toward joy. That was it. What I had been working so hard to learn for myself was a skill set that I could now help to teach others. I remembered my research on wellness and its eight dimensions. I thought: why not focus on that? Between my academic training, clinical experience, personal discoveries and newfound inner peace, I certainly had a lot to share with the world about what helps and what hurts on our individual and collective paths to health and happiness. And the more research that I did, the more that I realized just how many people could stand to benefit from that type of help. There are so many living without the joy that we each deserve, that is available to us; but we are so rarely taught how to access it. That was what I wanted to help others learn to do. It was perfect! Promoting wellness was my Ikigai!

Promoting myself, however, was another task altogether. Marketing was never my strong suit, but I did know some basics. I illustrated a logo, developed a tag line, revised my website and built up my social media presence. Between that and a solid text/email campaign to everyone I knew, I was officially in operation - ready to start living my dreams in January of 2015. Or so I thought.

"Ok, I'm ready dreams...come true," I thought. I will admit that there was a piece of me that just expected the flood gates of opportunity to open now that I had finally committed to this path. And in some ways, they did. But on other fronts, the process was slower than I would have hoped. I could feel that great things were coming, but I had no clue what shape they would take nor did I know when they might arrive and the sheer vulnerability of it all just freaked me out.

I applied for an online teaching job and was called the very next day to start right away. That was great. Convinced that the universe was conspiring in my favor, I submitted myself to writing jobs: Nothing! Then I was called to begin a wellness training contract that I proposed some months earlier and I thought, okay, it's all coming together now. So, I submitted my poetry to a major magazine for publication: Rejection; and so on and so on. In fact, the first year was filled with so many starts and stops that I sometimes wondered if I had done the right thing. Although to be honest, when you consider the years of doubt and emotional resistance that I had built up around these dreams, it's a wonder that I saw any moves at all in the first year... so I considered that a win.

I pushed forward with the understanding that it was going to take time to build this vision. I also knew that one of the best ways to bring it to fruition, was to continue doing the things that brought me the most joy. I didn't need them to be commissioned by others, paid for by others or otherwise validated by others. I just kept doing what I do. I kept publishing my monthly blog, working on the book manuscript, drawing and drafting other projects. I offered trainings and workshops, taught a number of classes and even started my own YouTube channel. I meditated and worked out, gratitude listed, travelled, and found ways to be kind to others. I stayed positive, I stayed focused, I had fun and I relaxed. And little by little, more and more of the vision manifested until I experienced joy in my every day. Not every dream that I ever dreamt had come to pass; I suspect that will never be the case since I dream a new dream each time it begins to look like an old dream might come true. I live in joy because I have learned to see the beauty in all I do and because I have created the space in my life to do those things which speak to my spirit the greatest kindness. I answered the call.

~ Research & Wrap-Up ~

Clearly, it's important to find ways to love what you do. Boehm and Lyubomirsky (2008) report that:

> Taken together, evidence from cross-sectional, longitudinal, and experimental studies supports the hypothesis that positive affect can bring about successful outcomes in the workplace. Happy people are more satisfied with their jobs and report having greater autonomy in their duties. They perform better on assigned tasks than their less happy peers and are more likely to take on extra role tasks such as helping others. They receive more social support from their coworkers and tend to use more cooperative approaches when interacting with others. (p.10)

It is equally important to do the things that you love to do. As we see in the work of Rottinghaus and Conrath (2009):

> Numerous factors contribute to job satisfaction and addressing the overall degree of fit between interests and work environments has been emphasized in vocational theory, research, and practice. (p.205) This study provided further support for the power of matching individuals' interests and occupational characteristics in determining satisfaction. (p.208)

That said, for me as for many others, nothing beats the satisfaction and fulfillment you feel, when you answer your calling – when you build a profession based in purpose. Duffy and Dik (2013) confirm that:

> ...viewing one's career as a calling is linked with a host of positive work and well-being criterion variables. These include, but are not limited to, heightened levels of career maturity, career commitment, work meaning, job satisfaction, life meaning, and life satisfaction. The link of calling to these variables is especially pronounced when people are living out their calling at work, and numerous in-depth qualitative studies have highlighted how the lives of individuals doing so are extremely meaningful and fulfilling. (p.434)

So, try loving what you do, doing what you love and answering your calling, as ways to balance your career and improve your occupational wellness.

5.

Align Your Pockets

Suggestions:
Invest in Yourself,
Save For a Sunny Day &
Believe in Abundance

A large part of the serenity and success that I've experienced is due, not only to the work I've put forth and the faith I've let in, but also to the many investments that I made in myself throughout the years. I don't think that I consciously understood the value of those investments at the time, but somehow, some way, I always knew that, no matter the cost, growing my mind and healing my spirit were worthwhile expenditures.

It's important to keep that perspective, because we live in a world where so many things are constantly competing for our resources. Money, in particular, is one of those resources that can feel scarce at times; we strive to preserve it, sometimes at the cost of our wellness. Yet, there is perhaps no more worthwhile spending than on experiences that improve our wellbeing. After all, what could be more important than rejuvenating and expanding. So, over the many years that I walked this path, I made sure to constantly, invest in myself, spending in three specific areas that proved invaluable: education, relaxation and adventure.

For instance, what others have absorbed in mortgage costs, I paid in tuition to become better educated and a greater thinker (which is pretty appropriate considering the years that I spent living in my head). And though I'm spending a lot of time these days learning how to stop my thoughts, I could not be more grateful for their existence and their complexity. I cherish my BA, MA, PhD and certifications very much. Not because of their supposed prestige or because they ushered me in to some upper echelon of society (I never much fit in with scholars and academics). I treasure my academic training because it taught me how to learn: how to live in curiosity, how to seek out answers, how to evaluate the validity and reliability of an idea (whether in my mind or that of others), and how to work, diligently, toward completing a worthwhile task. The process was that transformative. Not to mention, the impact of the content: the way I better understood society and how I learned to understand myself. Even the way that my education and training positioned me to secure teaching and training jobs and to pursue flexible high-paying work; it all validated the worth of that investment. A formal education is not always necessary for others to build these skills, but I'd be lying if I said that it didn't help to build these skills in me and others' confidence in me.

Another investment in myself that always proved fruitful was money spent on relaxation. Whether I was booking a deep tissue massage at $110 a pop, or simply blowing $5 on aromatherapy oils, the result was a reduction in stress, which led to my being more open to great opportunities, more creative and more focused when I got back to a task. I know that many carry around a guilt associated with doing these things, because "there's so much to do" and "so many others to care for." I get it. I have also felt it. It's easy to believe thoughts like, "who am I to have this when others don't" or "there are so many other things that I could be doing right now," or "every minute or dollar spent on myself is one that I should be spending on my child/parent/partner." But I've learned that taking care of myself always makes me better, not just for myself but for others as well: kinder, more responsive, more energetic. I am a better version of myself, when I've tended to my needs... And sometimes I have to pay for that, and it's money well-spent.

While we're at this recap of financial investments that have fed my soul (education, self-care), let us not forget to also add travel. I heard that most Americans spend 25-30% of their income on housing. I was spending more like 10-15% and reallocating the remaining funds to adventurous vacations. What can I say? I enjoy going far to meet people I would not otherwise encounter: see how we're different, see how we're similar and get a better understanding of other cultures. I thoroughly enjoy experiencing the natural resources available overseas: different climates and smells, beaches and rain forests, foods and landscapes, and the animals. Nothing was more invigorating than riding a camel in Morocco, joking with monkeys in Spain, being carried through the rivers of Thailand on the backs of elephants, kissing dolphins in Mexico or snorkeling with an array of beautiful fish in Bermuda. It's humbling beyond words to see yourself among the many splendors that source has created. I regret no dollar spent or penny dropped on foreign land, for what I gained from each visit has changed me profoundly. In the end, it is important to invest in the experiences that make us who we are. For who we are is the greatest gift that we can give the world.

That is not to say that I do not believe in saving money. In fact, I dare say that one of the things that helped me feel comfortable initiating the transition to consultant/entrepreneur was having a savings account. I couldn't have predicted that I would get a teaching job and a training contract in year one. In fact, I had no real/realistic expectation for what year one would look like at all. So, when I started to play with the thought of going out on my own, I immediately began to put more and more money away to ensure that I had a cushion on which to land when I finally did take that leap. I knew there would be things that I would want to buy and places that I would want to go, and I didn't want to feel deprived and thus regretful of my decision to take that leap. You've heard of people saving for a rainy day? Well, I needed an account to continue to finance my many sunny days. So, I began to save.

I've always been pretty frugal. Some might even call me "cheap." I do rather like the finer things in life, I just don't like spending the finer part of my check to enjoy them. So, I walk into stores and go directly to the clearance racks in the back. I vacation on off-peak season and I spend an inordinate amount of time on the web searching for the best price on an item that I want. I've always been the kind of girl that preferred 4 pairs of $50 heels to any $200 pair of stilettos. And as far as I was concerned, $50 was splurging. At this point, it's pretty second nature for me, to scout for a deal. I like to get the biggest bang for my buck. Call it my sport of choice.

Perhaps, it's because I was taught the value of a dollar by hard working parents and humble beginnings. Or, maybe it's because I'm very independent, and I like knowing that I have something to fall back on, should I need to. Whatever the reason, that healthy respect for the vastness of money's potential stuck with me way into the six-figure income that I was about to walk away from.

Especially now, with my eye on the prize that was living my dreams, I was keeping my spending to a minimum. While my friends went out and bought BMWs, I leased a Kia and splurged for the 4-wheel drive and heated seats (I mean, it was New York after all). I loved the luxury apartments that some of my peers enjoyed: indoor pools and 24-hour concierge services. Still I stayed in the basement studio of that Northeast Bronx apartment house and just decorated it like a day spa. The girls wanted to hang? I was over it - every drink was $15, parking for the night was $50 and even the diner bill afterward seemed too high for the omelette with home fries that I ordered. Plus, I was tired of going out anyway.

I had some serious expenses that I couldn't reduce: student loans, rent, the car payment, insurance. But what modesty I could live with, I implemented. And I reallocated any money that I could spare to my savings account for the adventure that I knew was soon to come. I tried not to deprive myself too much, for fear that I'd grow resentful. If I really wanted to meet my cousin at that little French bistro we loved, I did so. If I felt an impulse toward a gift for my parents or the need to see a movie or play, I went for it. But I let splurging be the exception and made saving the rule.

In fact, I was shocked at all of the ways that I was able to trim the fat in my monthly budget; packing simple lunches that took little time and cost little money: oatmeal, soup or cottage cheese for instance. I put all of my bills on auto-pay which meant no more late fees. I cut my gift budget in half and got more creative with present ideas for birthdays and other special occasions. I didn't drive any more than I needed to and proactively filled my tank at the most reasonably priced quality stations.

Most importantly, I stayed financially focused on what the funds were for. My savings would have to stretch to cover marketing materials, travel, conference registrations and other start-up costs until the business picked up. It also had to be enough to take care of my personal expenses (rent, car, etc.) until some work came in. That financial uncertainty was, perhaps, the most anxiety inducing piece of this whole ordeal; knowing that I had only six to twelve months of savings on which to live was incredibly scary. It put a dangerously pressure-filled timeline on my strive for success. Many insisted that I should have stayed in executive management longer, built a bigger egg nest, had more to fall back on. But I learned long ago not to let perfection become the enemy of progress. You can get stuck in the rut for a long time awaiting the perfect circumstances for your fantasy exit. I knew that if I stayed under the pretense of saving "enough" to leave, the money would never reach "enough" and I would eventually become unhappy. So, I left with roughly 9 months' worth of savings and tried to keep from focusing on when the money would run out and focused instead on the abundance of blessings that were awaiting me.

That too was key, changing my ideas and thoughts about money. See, one of the byproducts of growing up in modest economic conditions is that you become all too familiar with feelings of scarcity. "There's not enough." There's not enough of this, there's not enough of that. Add water to the orange juice that's going low, find the cheapest gas station, it's a game of financial survival and my parents had gotten very good at playing it. Like the child of many parents working all too hard for a dollar, I grew up witnessing uncomfortable conversations about the household finances and watching my parents sacrifice things that they may have wanted or needed, to get me things. They were very fiscally responsible and taught me to be as well. My mother was the accounting type – document every penny. She taught me to keep track of the dollars. My father was the resourceful type – could fix anything you may have thought needed replacing. He showed me how to stretch the dollars. Between the two of them, I was well prepared to make a dollar out of fifteen cents, as the adage says. And it served me very well as I grew into adulthood. I was always able to do a lot with a little, which helped me to be very financially independent and a budget mastermind at work.

The problem, however, was that my skilled ability to make a dollar out of fifteen cents, was sponsored by the idea that there were only fifteen cents. It was a talent born of flawed thinking, and a thinking that was motivated by fear. I could have, should have, easily approached it from the position of, "let me be creative, because I only have access to fifteen cents in this very moment," and understood that was no indication of the abundance available to me at other moments. But instead I took it to mean that fifteen cents was all there ever was/all there would ever be, all there could ever be. And so, even though I studied, and played lotto, and pursued big salary jobs, there was a piece of me that, deep down inside, believed it could never really happen for me. After all, fifteen cents doesn't leave much when divided amongst the 7 billion people on earth.

I wasn't completely crazy in my rationale either. I was a woman of color and a sociologist, which meant extensive training in inequality: racism, sexism, classism - redlining, the wage gap, the alleged culture of poverty. Everywhere I turned, the same message seemed to be shouted from history and research - there's not enough and what little there is will not be available to you.

So even though I worked, and I prayed to live in monetary abundance, it was all under the pretense that financial stability was essentially unattainable. The problem is, that I was largely unaware, that by thinking this way, I was making it so. I didn't necessarily believe in the power of my thoughts to create my reality. I thought of my thoughts as simple observations of my reality. And so, the more that I convinced myself of wealth's unattainability, the more unattainable it was.

Why was I so convinced that there wasn't enough? I remember hearing that Global wealth rose to $241 trillion in 2013. So there certainly was enough. Why was I so convinced that there wasn't enough for me? What made those who had it any more worthy, lucky, capable than me? Nothing. The truth is that when my thoughts were connected to social systems, I felt limited to the potential of those social systems, and those systems had proven to be oppressive and untrustworthy such that things weren't looking so great for me. But when I felt connected to source energy through faith, gratitude and mindfulness, I was no longer bound by the likelihood of events happening as predicted by historical trends. I felt strong, powerful, like I could achieve anything. Surely, I had made this too personal, thinking that I was being locked out of wealth, when I have as much claim to it as anyone: operating on the same energy as everyone, sharing a source with those who access wealth easily, openly and frequently. I had now come to believe that it was just as available to me.

Like everything else, we walk through the world collecting evidence to support what we already believe. When I believed that there wasn't enough, there never was. All I constantly saw around me was lack and need. Even the people who surrounded me tended to be broke all the time and complaining about money problems. When I started to believe in abundance, not just of money, but of opportunity, of kindness and of inspiration, things really started to change.

~ Research & Wrap-Up ~

There are probably no better investments than those you make on yourself – your values, your interests and your betterment. Matz, Gladstone and Stillwell (2016) agree that:

> …spending provides the greatest increase in happiness and well-being when it is on goods and services that match consumers' personalities. (p.2)

Still, you may opt not to spend. You may choose to save instead. If so, consider saving with the intention to fund a sunny day. After all, the research of De Francisco Vela, Casais, and Desmet (2014) shows that it will make your saving experience a much more meaningful one:

> From the studies we conclude that design can contribute to the meaningfulness of saving, by

enabling users to set up an intention, visualize it, and empathize with it. (p.69)

Thankfully, spending and saving are not mutually exclusive. There is enough in this world for you to do both. So, feel free to believe in abundance. A report released by Bain and Company, Inc. (2012) asserts that:

Today, total financial assets are nearly 10 times the value of the global output of all goods and services. Our analysis leads us to conclude that for the balance of the decade, markets will generally continue to grapple with an environment of capital superabundance... Moreover, as financial markets in China, India and other emerging economies continue to develop their own financial sectors, total global capital will expand by half again, to an estimated $900 trillion by 2020. (p.3)

So, try investing in yourself, saving for a sunny day and believing in abundance, as ways to align your pockets and improve your financial wellness.

6.

Strengthen Your Connections

Suggestions:
Be Honest,
Picky &
Vulnerable

Of course I wasn't the only one who invested in me. By this point, I had built a supportive network of friends and family, who genuinely believed in my potential, respected my choices and were willing and able to demonstrate their support of me. That last part was key.

You see, I had been loved by a number of people in my past, for whom the relationship was simply defined by me doing all of the supporting. It was my fault really. As in my romantic relationships, here too, I had set up this dynamic with many friends and family. I was "the responsible one," the one with all of the answers and all of the power, the "rescuer," the "fixer." Part of it was, frankly, a bit of survivor's guilt. I had found ways to be happy and felt like I didn't deserve it unless I brought everyone to joy with me. I suppose part of it was also ego. I knew what worked and I had to show them. Another piece of it, I'm sure, was tied up in feelings of debt. My family and friends had played such a huge role in who I was, and I tended to confuse being grateful, with owing them something. Whatever the case, I certainly found myself in some exhausting friendships (even familial ones) over the years.

There was the lending of money, which always gets old quick; and the keeping of secrets I shouldn't have even known. There were the many explanations that I felt compelled to give, for choices that I had every right to make, and the tireless requests for advice about situations that they clearly weren't ready to get out of. There were times I felt like "who am I to...," and times when I screamed "you have no right to...," and there was so much of me compensating for what they couldn't or wouldn't do. I remember it like it was yesterday, the enmeshment and codependency and mostly the draining feeling I would get in my chest when they stepped in the room or said hello on the other end of the phone. It was how I felt when I knew that she was about to ask for a favor, or that he was about to spend the next 40 minutes painting himself as the victim of something that he wouldn't/couldn't admit that he was causing.

In fact, I get tired even thinking about just how many of those relationships I had in my life - all with people that I know loved me very much. Some of whom still do. But I had spent so much of my life being "independent," and looking like I had it together, that I had forgotten to teach others that my needs were important too. Heck, I had forgotten to mention that I even had needs.

Then my 30s hit and the spiritual evolution really started to speed up. I discovered that, not only did I have needs in my nonromantic relationships that were not being met, I had preferences and desires and negotiables and non-negotiables, just like in my romantic relationships. And just like in my romantic relationships, they were important to honor. I started to understand that the way that others treated me was a direct representation of how I felt about myself; that they only saw my needs as important as I saw them and valued my ideas as much as I valued them. And if I was running around prioritizing their needs, I couldn't have thought myself very important at all. But now, things were changing. I was loving myself more and living with a greater sense of self directed interest; not an arrogance of sorts, just a more intense connection with my worth. And it was time for my friendships (including familial ones) to catch up. I made three major changes that made the difference. I became more honest, more picky and more vulnerable.

It's not that I had been intentionally lying to my friends and family, you see. I had always told them what I thought was true (speaking my mind was never a struggle). But on my path to self-discovery, I had now learned that things that I thought were true, were not. Or perhaps my truths had changed. No need to figure out which was which, the important thing was that I was now keenly aware of my needs and wants, and limits, and it was time that my friends and family were too; because I did mind lending the money, and I did mind being spoken to in a nasty way, and I did mind being the one who always went out of her way. The days of pretending that I was an endless supply of emotional and financial resources available for them to tap into at whim, were over. The truth (new or newfound) was that a few of my relationships were just not fulfilling enough to help me replenish at a rapid enough rate to make up for the way they were depleting me.

I was freaking exhausted. I had to change. So, I did. And when my friends and family asked why things were changing, or brought up the changes, I began to tell them why. And when it was appropriate, I took full responsibility for having set the precedent, and for the years that I made it seem like we were cool when I was secretly annoyed and underfed on the inside; or the months since I had outgrown the things that we used to do together and my endlessly trying to convince myself that we could still hang out. And if the situation merited it, I apologized for my critical and controlling ways, which had ever so cleverly developed out of my "I am the savior" mentality. And in some cases, I explained that I would end up resenting him/her if I continued the way that I had been going, so I had to make some changes and I trusted that our friendship could survive it and come out stronger on the other end. And in other cases, I simply stopped going out of my way and watched as some relationships just dissipated without the effort that I had long been putting in to keep them afloat (I suppose that had been one of my fears all along). I'm talking everything from, "I'm not going to make it to your event," to "No, you can't hide out in my apartment while the cops are looking for you" (true story). The "Nos" just started to fly out of my mouth.

I made a conscious effort to be true to what I needed to be happy and healthy and to connect with people who were making choices to do what they needed to do to be happy and healthy too; and who chose me and my wellbeing, as I was choosing them. And I watched as many of my friends and family just filtered right out. And it was hard. The conversations were tough. The ones where there was no conversation were tougher. It was as if a tornado had hit and wiped out all of my social life. All that was left was cellphone contacts where friendships used to be. But in the end, that cleansing proved a healthy and necessary one. When the dust settled, and the debris cleared, I realized that I had a more solid support system than I had ever imagined. In the crowds of loving acquaintances that never fully connected and needy pals that over-connected, stood a committee of truly perfect souls whose purpose was a great fit with mine; whose love had never dwindled. They, too, grew as I grew, and adjusted as I adjusted, and had dug their heels into the ground during the storm. And their value, which I may have taken for granted over the years, was ever so much more clearly revealed as the fog lifted.

In the place of many who were gone, with whom I once shared a friendship, came others whose visions of themselves, the world and me were more aligned with the joy I now knew life to be. Now that I had much less ego invested in being a "savior," I had also stopped attracting victims. Now that I respected my worth, I had begun attracting friends and developing closer relationships with existing acquaintances and family members who felt similarly about me, and about themselves. Now that I was in a place of understanding the importance of equality and reciprocity in friendships, I was more wisely choosing those with whom to engage.

Boy, did being picky work out for me! In so many ways my life is more fulfilling as a result of my being more discriminating with my time, emotions and energy. In fact, energy in and of itself is one of the salient pieces of this puzzle. The energy that a person carries with them can be so contagious. And while I am sure that it is true that positive energy can drown out and/or transform negative energy, I'm fairly certain that it takes a great deal of effort for even a positive person not to be affected by the negativity of someone with whom they feel truly connected. Just like in my romantic relationships, I had hoped to do more transforming of the negative than absorbing of the negative. And just like in my romantic relationships, that very need to change others rather than focus on my own growth, was an indication of my fragility. And that fragility made it more likely that their negativity would impact me sooner and more greatly than I could ever impact them. The best way out, was to save myself and show some damn respect for their journeys and how they chose to travel them. So that's what I did. And I can't tell you the relief that I felt not being surrounded by the negative energy that they brought with them, or that my resistance to their lifestyles brought to our friendship. It felt good to steer clear of the complaining, the paralysis and the unhappiness that many of them inhabited, and to feel free from judging them, helping them or in anyway being responsible for, or affected by, them.

It was so nice to enjoy the company of acquaintances, friends and family who were like-minded; deliberately healing, growing and evolving. The room felt light when they entered. We laughed more. We were better to ourselves when we hung out: better to our bodies, more useful of our minds, more conscious of our spirits. And before I knew it, between the old greats, newbies and transformed constants, I had built a network of support unmatched in power.

When I made the decision to follow my heart and pursue my dreams, I propelled to success in no small part due to their respective investments in me. I was in a place of transition and change is never easy. I had to find a way to minimize my risk, while maximizing my exposure, and for a control freak, like I used to be, that took nothing short of a miracle. But now, in the hands of such capable people, and with a lot of ego work, I finally felt comfortable being vulnerable. I could now admit that I was not as happy as I wished to be, that I had a few ideas about how I could be happier and that I was going to need all of the help that I could get.

Surely, I figured that there would be some positive response from those with which I remained uber close. After all, I had always done my best to be kind to them, available and more of a resource than a drain. I didn't demand the same in return, but I more or less anticipated it, because I knew they too were kind, giving people who cared for me. What I did not anticipate was how many people there were whose great generosity would push me forward. Some provided me with shelter, food and light so I could write at 3:24am when inspiration hit. Others flooded me with referrals that helped launch my business. Some hired me outright for any number of tasks: writing, training, coaching. A number of them kept my spirits up with lunch dates, shopping trips and fun outings. One edited. Another prayed. When I got arrogant, someone called me out on my self-righteousness. When I overworked, I was reminded to take a moment.

My very real need to feel connected to a community of people was being met with a massive amount of support on their part. And I did everything that I could to return the favors: I cleaned, and babysat, and cooked and tutored, and counseled and chauffeured, and bought gifts and gave discounts, and all with a smile (most of the time). And I never felt indebted, because they never expected anything in return.

I felt honored and humbled, having been touched and inspired by their kindness. And I learned the difference between gratitude and indebtedness. Gratitude is what you are blessed to feel when you are supported by beings who are full on the inside and whose feelings for you reflect that. Indebtedness is what you are expected to feel when you are supported by beings who are empty on the inside and whose feelings for you reflect that.

My life was no longer full of the latter, only the former, and I considered myself fortunate to have such a solid system of support. I had taken a leap of faith and found that I was not only carried through the air by the soft cushiony magic carpet of savings that I had prepared, but by the rich network of positive people that had webbed together to support me.

I'm still a little startled and embarrassed now, when I think of the pride that I used to take in saying that I had done something on my own. It was so important to me to feel independent. The truth is that, now that I've done some soul searching, I know that I've never truly done anything on my own. Source energy has always been with me. And I've always had the benefit of being connected to an excess of people who took an interest in me. Family, friends, colleagues, mentors and teachers, on whom I have always been able to depend, and for whom I have made myself available... and together we do more, and we do better!

~ Research & Wrap-Up ~

I guess the lesson here is to just be honest. A study by Brinke, Lee and Carney (2015) suggests that:

> ...telling the truth, being altruistic, acting fairly and being generally other-oriented are virtues directly linked to a suite of positive health outcomes such as: better health and physical wellness, lower stress, decreased cellular aging, increased psychological wellbeing and longevity of life. (p.180)

It also helps to be picky about who and what surrounds you, even if that means spending some time alone. In fact, sometimes being alone can help to get you get clear. In their work, Gardner and Steinberg (2005) found that:

> ...individuals may take more risks, evaluate risky behavior more positively, and make more risky decisions when they are with their peers than when they are by themselves. (p.632)

As important, is allowing yourself to be vulnerable. It can be so difficult for us to ask for help. Mostly, because we are so scared that we will not get it. The work of Flynn and Bohns (2008) reminds us that if we ask, we will likely receive:

> We find that people generally underestimate the likelihood of compliance in making a direct request for help, in part, because they fail to fully appreciate that although it is difficult for help seekers to risk rejection, it is also difficult for potential helpers to offer rejection. Recognizing and overcoming this paralyzing, and in many cases unfounded, fear may bear meaningful consequences, not just for individuals but for the good deeds they hope to accomplish. (p.28)

So, try being honest, picky and vulnerable, as ways to strengthen your connections and improve your social wellness.

7.

Honor Your Body

Suggestions:
Stay Nourished,
Active &
Well-Rested

N eedless to say, with my shift in energy, my success
and my support, I was feeling like a million bucks;
and not just on the inside either. I was in the best
physical shape I had experienced since adolescence. Even
some of the health issues that I discovered in my 20s (asthma,
heart murmur, high cholesterol) had since disappeared.
Current medical exams showed no sign of them. It was as if
their diagnosis never occurred. Somehow, on the path to
healing my spirit and growing my mind, I had also managed to
better my body. And what a difference that betterment was
making. My energy level was off the charts. My strength and
agility were remarkable, and I was full of vitality.

It's hard to pinpoint what exactly caused the shift. I'd like
to say that it was this or that, but I suppose my heightened
physical wellness came as the result of a series of choices and
changes I made in my early 30s. While I had always tried to be
good to myself (no drugs or intentional self-harm), I became
even more health conscious, entering my fourth decade of life;
more conscious of what I put in my body and more mindful
of what I did with it.

Perhaps it started with my saying "no" to meat. See, part of
my spiritual journey had led me to question the mass breeding
and killing of animals for food consumption. I didn't like what
I learned: factory farming, hormones, worldwide massive food
waste. But above all, I was a lifetime animal lover, who on

some level, always struggled with the idea of animals being killed for food. So, I stopped eating beef, pork and chicken first and then progressed from pescetarianism (still ate fish) to vegetarianism (no meat at all). The transition eliminated a large amount of animal fat from my diet, which in and of itself had a great impact on my body. It also really helped me to vastly increase my fruit and vegetable intake and I started to use vitamins to compensate for the resulting change in my iron and protein intake. I was feeling great.

The downside, though, now that meat was off my menu, was that I started to eat a lot more carb-rich side dishes when I was out. No one needs that much sugar in their system, so now I'm working on letting go of potatoes, rice, bread and pasta. It is still hard. But meat I don't miss. Of course, it was quite an adjustment at first, to be in Times Square and not eat one of those hot dogs that you buy from a cart. You know, the ones you savor while trying to distract your mind from what's truly inside them. It sounds disgusting, but almost any New Yorker would kill for the comforting taste of a NYC hot dog. Going out to eat with friends was slightly more challenging, as I often found myself combining appetizers and sides to try and make an entree. And holidays were even harder. After all, no Latino family holiday celebration is quite complete without roast pork and *pasteles* filled with meat. My will was certainly tested. But I was firm in my decision and the longer I held steadfastly to my convictions, the more time I gave my palate to transform, until the taste of meat no longer held a monopoly on satisfaction. I began to enjoy a portobello mushroom the way that I had once treasured a steak. And I felt better, proud even.

So, a few years later, I decided to say "no" to alcohol as well. Though I never considered myself to have a drinking problem (not that people with a problem ever do), I had certainly found myself drinking more and more as a part of partying more and more. Following the divorce and related depression, I had taken to going out to dance clubs with my cousins on Friday nights. Then, we added Saturday nights to the schedule. Soon, we were hanging out at lounges on Thursday nights as well, and on Sundays we found an all-day happy hour restaurant, or an outdoor bar in the summer.

Each night would start the same. Someone would buy a round of drinks for the group of pretty girls that just walked in the place. Then one of us would buy the second to return the favor. Then a third. Even with my limiting myself to three, I was still consuming more liquor than a healthy body could want. And that was just that one night. Multiply it by the four nights that a single, childless, financially stable girl, who loves to dance (like me), is likely to hit the club each week and what was not an alcohol problem, could become a problem, quick. Add to that the crazy food choices at the diner after the club, the hours lost sleeping and recuperating the next day and the questionable romantic judgment that kicked in, in the dark, with a drink in hand, and I had a lengthy list of compelling reasons to rethink this very unhelpful habit I had picked up.

Why was I drinking so much anyway? I didn't need it to have fun, I was always the first one on the dance floor, alcohol or not. Plus, I was pretty uninhibited when I was sober – said what I thought, did what I wanted – a natural part of my personality. Drinking that much certainly wasn't helping me to achieve any of the many goals that I was setting for myself, nor was it helping me through the very hard work that I was committed to pursuing. In fact, partying this much wasn't helping anything at all. So, one day, I went out with the girls, one of which offered me a glass of wine. I replied, "no thanks, I'm not drinking today." Clearly bewildered, she exclaimed, "What, why?" It may sound silly, but that's the moment that I knew things were going to have to change. "I should need a reason to drink," I thought; to alter my mood and poison my liver. Yet, somehow, I had found myself in a lifestyle where I had to give a reason NOT to drink. What was I doing? The norms of the past years just weren't consistent with who I now wanted to be. They weren't consistent with the best version of me. Something had to change. Again, I had to change. So, in the six years since, I have never again picked up another drink. I've yet to regret making that decision. And I suspect that I never will.

As a result, the constant hanging out also lessened. Now that I was sober all the time, the clubs and lounges were less fun than they had once been. I smelled everything: the mix of perfume scents, the sweat, vodka on the breath of that guy that kept asking me to dance. I became less tolerant of the crowds and the constant bumping. And what to say of how easily annoyed I became with the one or two of my friends who always had one or two, too many. Sigh. I wasn't a good fit with club culture anymore and my friends and family did not need me there judging and making them uncomfortable. So that changed too: no more drinking or hanging in the clubs all night. Time to be more deliberate in the way I used my energy.

Hanging out less also helped me with another physical wellness goal that it was time to take more seriously: rest. I was quite busy with work, school and other projects throughout those years. I needed much more sleep than I was getting on the weekdays and now that my weekend crying fits and depressive episodes had begun to wane, Saturdays and Sundays had to be a time for restorative sleep. The one thing that my body definitely did not need was me trying to find "love in the club" until 4am, only to hit the diner afterwards. I was fatigued, which has been proven to be the cognitive functioning equivalent of intoxicated (explaining some of my dating choices at the time). My physical vitality was in danger and the only thing that would revitalize it was a massive lifestyle transformation.

That epiphany ushered in the very easy release of yet another unhealthy little habit that I had picked up: cigars. I never smoked cigarettes, but I had developed an affinity for the taste and calm of a mild corona or panatela. I knew, even back when I tried my first, that it wasn't good for me. But I liked the smell, the look, the taste and the feel, so I occasionally lit one up. That is until the summer of 2014, when I finally decided that, pursuant to the new guidelines of my life of wellness, I would have to quit. No more cognac coated Dominicans fresh out of the humidor. The days of sitting in a cigar lounge, on my cousin's deck or atop the outdoor benches of City Island's fast-food, seafood restaurants, had come to an end. I could no longer justify inhaling a heightened level of Nitrosamines because I liked to savor the smoke's sweet burn. So, I quit.

I had become so good at quitting things that were bad for me, that quitting this wasn't nearly as difficult as I thought that it would be. In fact, the sacrificing of unhealthy habits came much more naturally to me now that I was on this new path to wellness. And I felt all the better for it. I was learning, growing, feeling more peace within myself. I could feel my insides more still, my brain less busy, my spirit more alive. It was working. All of these changes; they were working. I was getting stronger, more focused, less fragile. I was becoming a better version of me. It was great. Still, it was going to take more than abstinence from meat, alcohol and tobacco to get my body right and I knew that.

I was aware that lifestyle changes are not simply about stopping the problem behaviors, but also about introducing healthy habits in a consistent way. So, I began to bring more physical activity into my every day to help build on what I was doing; starting with yoga. It was an interest of mine since I became exposed to its power through my readings and research on meditation. I found it difficult to get to the classes with my taxing management schedule, so I ordered a number of videos and practiced at home. I downloaded the app and snuck poses in at work during a break and I got to a class when I could. It's astonishing just how many different types of yoga there are: Bikram in the heat; Yin Yoga for the joints; Sivananda, if you're interested in chanting and scripture study; and the list goes on. All beautiful and sacred, I found myself drawn to different traditions depending on what I was seeking and what energy I would bring to it. So, I varied the types I tried and enjoyed what each had to offer. And for years, I've done exactly that: kept yoga a ritual through which I center my mind, reconnect to my energy and rejuvenate my body, using various poses, approaches and intensities. I'm still far from mastering a few difficult poses (e.g. one-legged king pigeon pose) and I may never advance to a headstand or dragonfly, but who cares? What's important is that I have found ways to keep my body active and in shape and yoga helped me do that.

I also started walking. At first it was on the $320 treadmill that I bought and assembled (I still wonder about those extra screws they sent). I set it up right next to my bed, facing the television set, and I began to walk at a snail's pace. After all, I had never been a very fit/active individual. I played no sports. I had no athletic hobbies. I didn't even know how to ride a bike for goodness sake. So, the thought of working out, or walking briskly, very rarely crossed my mind. That is, until I started to see the weight pile on. Those carbs were doing a number on me. I was feeling sluggish, and even more, I learned that people that exercised regularly were likely to live much longer. I thought to myself, "get off your butt Dinorah... You can do this." At first, I walked 3.5 miles, once or twice per week, at a 3.0 speed. Now, I walk 5 miles per day, at a 3.6/3.8 speed, while watching Downton Abbey on my iPad. I find there's no better way to get lost in a workout, legs carrying you against the power of the belt and tension toning those arms, than an hour and a half of drama pulling you into the screen. It's so entertaining that you forget you're in motion - the greatest distraction. And since there are certain shows that I will only watch on the treadmill, wanting to see the next episode also becomes a great source of motivation.

Walking on the treadmill really got me into the habit of staying active, pushing my body and keeping myself fit. At first, it was tough to get myself in gear, but eventually I started to like the way I felt when I finished a walk, and not just on the treadmill either. I started to walk around the neighborhoods where I found myself and I began walking to more of the places to which I needed to go. I took extra laps around the mall and soon, I was even hiking. It was one of those things that I thought I'd never do. Born in the Bronx, raised in Yonkers, "I'm a city girl – a concrete jungle New Yorker," I always thought to myself. I don't do hiking, or camping, or any of those other activities that women are doing right before they get murdered at the start of scary movies. I had always kept my behind where there are streetlights and concrete paths already paved specifically so I might walk on them. Until I went on my first hike... And fell in love!

There is something so profoundly touching about the vast beauty of nature. Nothing shrinks your ego back to size like standing beside a colossal mountain or watching the way multiple species of animals play together in the valley's ponds. I've never seen so many shades of green or heard so many birds call my name in different dialects and pitches. I was in awe at the oceans along this one trail that took me high and then low and allowed me to understand the pain and laughter in every cry of the waves crashing. It was majestic. I was humbled and distracted. By the time I finished walking the trail. I had already put in six miles worth of hike. I was hooked. How could I have been so wrong about such a lovely hobby. I was excited by hiking. Hiking made me excited about the world in which I lived - and I loved it. I loved feeling the freedom, the challenge and the joy that came with this sporty past time. I was losing weight, feeling good and loving life.

~ Research & Wrap-Up ~

How we treat our bodies is integral to our quality of life. So, let's watch what we put in them. The findings of a study by Khaw et al. (2008) support what my personal experiences taught me. Some behaviors are just not helpful to maximizing your potential:

> ...four health behaviors—not smoking, not being physically inactive, having a moderate alcohol intake, and having a high fruit and vegetable intake—were combined into a simple pragmatic four-item health behavior score... There was a strong trend of decreasing mortality risk with increasing number of positive health behaviors... (p.42)

One of the things that is helpful is physical activity. Szabo (2003) wrote:

> Research in epidemiology reveals that a physically active lifestyle yields numerous health benefits. Evidence also shows that physical activity is associated with positive mental wellbeing and reduced reactivity to cognitive stress. The mental benefits of chronic and acute exercise are the most prominent on measures of affect and anxiety. Acute exercise triggers immediate improvements in affect, which renders it a suitable antidote to the hassles and challenges of the everyday life, in addition to overcoming some ill effects of an increasingly sedentary lifestyle. (p.77)

Another way to honor your body is to give it adequate rest. The work of Walker (2009) points to the benefits of rest, not just for the body, but also for the mind:

> Beyond memory and plasticity, a growing number of human neuroscience studies, set on a foundation of

clinical insights, point to an exciting role for sleep in regulating affective brain function and emotional experience. (p.192)

So, try staying nourished, active and well-rested, as ways to honor your body and improve your physical wellness.

8.

Celebrate Your Surroundings

Suggestions:
Enjoy Nature,
Decorate to Inspire &
Live Free

The simple fact was that hiking allowed me to relish in nature's many gifts. As I walked, I noticed things that I had never quite noticed before. Citrusy tinges of sun that had left unique tan-lined tattoos on each leaf of every tree. A ground that seemingly came alive with the reach of each ray's warmth. Even the dirt below me seemed anointed with sublime bursts of joy. On my beachside hikes, the motion of the sea would just drown out my thoughts until only the chanting rhythms of each wave accompanied me through the trails of Pines and Palms. As I glanced up at the sky, I could feel my heart fill with shades of color unparalleled. There were more hues of blue reflected in the heavens than I had never dived in or drank from before. It was crystallized and comforting. It was so serene. It was so surreal. It allowed me a vaster appreciation for the greatness of this world that we've been given and helped me to open up my mind. This outdoors had become a new love of mine and I was suddenly aware of the years that its beauty had been missing from my life.

As I mentioned, we were city folk - my family and me. Your stereotypical New Yorkers, we viewed walking as a mode of transportation, not a scenic pastime. Living in urban communities, in inconsistent climates, made it easy to overlook a walk's healing properties. Everyone was working so hard to get where they were going (figuratively and literally), that stopping to smell the roses just wasn't on the agenda. Getting to your destination in time meant walking with a purpose - quickly and with little detour. Remember, we're talking the Bronx, New York, in the 1980s. Streets were overcrowded, nature was neglected, our air was polluted, cold on most days, and crime was skyrocketing. Walking wasn't efficient, it wasn't fun, and in many cases, it wasn't safe. In mid-1985 my mother learned of drugs being dealt out of the building where we were living and just like that, we were out of there.

My parents scraped together every penny they had saved and moved me from the Fordham Road vicinity, to the suburbs of Westchester County. Yonkers, New York was just 20 minutes outside of Manhattan, but as far as my parents were concerned, it was a world away. Joined by my grandparents, we settled into a one-family house and never looked back (that is until I returned to the Bronx following my marital separation). The new Yonkers neighborhood was much nicer. Walking back and forth to the bus stop was reasonably safe and lined with many more trees and cared-for front lawns than I was used to. Still, at this point, we just weren't outdoorsy kinds of people. Walking my backyard, to my swing-set, through the wildly growing blades of grass, that my working parents rarely had time to cut, was about as close to hiking as I got. It was decades before the joys of walking outdoors finally grew on me.

As an adult, I began to travel a lot. One delight emerged: long walks along the beaches of the Caribbean's many islands and on the streets of our world's many metro-cities. That kind of walking I had started to like. There was something intriguing about being in the midst of strangers as they carried on with their days. I liked creating stories in my mind about where they were headed or where they were coming from. I enjoyed smelling the various perfumes and colognes that colored our brushing moments (unlike my experience in the clubs). I took especially great pleasure in watching lovers hold hands and families share gut-sponsored laughs. Walking for sport pushed me into this space of respectful voyeurism that made my travel, and life in general, seem so much more vibrant. An experience of which I found myself becoming fond. The people, however, as fascinating as they were, paled in comparison to the relationship that I began to develop with the four elements of nature.

I had heard of mystic philosophies that posited the existence of four essential elements. I had also stayed barely awake enough through a high school science class to remember the four states of matter. Still, I felt no affinity toward either of these ideas over the years. Leave me indoors, I thought, more times than not. That is until I began to commune with nature on these outdoor walks of mine. Then my whole perspective changed. Each time I ventured outdoors, I could now feel a connection.

I could pass the time at lakes and ponds, rivers and oceans, or even just at the foot of a cataract, hypnotized by the majesty of its songs and dances. Water's (liquid) soft crashes and humming undertones served such a harmonious soundtrack to its pretty lifts and plunges. The way it flowed, with an unplanned plan, inspired so much faith in the perfection of things. Every drop unique and significant in its own right but made greater in its joining to a collective. I could see prophesies float to the surface in the rounded curves that were formed. It was simple, yet profound. And that was just the view. Submerging myself into its depths felt all the more healing. Each and every time, I emerged feeling younger and freer, as if I had bathed in a mythical fountain thought to preserve the innocence of my spirit.

Above, the sun (fire/plasma) kissed my skin. It was the safest I had ever felt. Illuminated by its light, comforted by its heat; I closed my eyes in its strongest moments and just felt as its glow penetrated my aura. The unmistakable transfer of energy was so evident to me now. How long I had longed for it without the slightest understanding of its power to restore and rejuvenate. My heart felt dainty in its hold. My skin honeyed in response. Every inch of me paused, cradled by its warm caress. I was often left paralyzed by its fierce attention. How stinging goodness could be. I felt a gasp come on. My breath was lost in the marvel and there I stood, lovingly overwhelmed by the blaze. Then, just as it could begin to seem unbearable, there would be a breeze gifted by the trees or brought in by the waves.

Instantly, I could once again breathe, so effortlessly. Wind (air/gas) cleansing me, carrying with it the memory of places just visited and stories left in the past. Its invisible might always shaking me to the core - a great reminder that a great force is not always foreseeable. I could lose myself in the patience it inspires or the way it combed through my curls. I love that it dries the tears it brings to my eyes, with each motion solving any problem it created. It's so consuming and yet so removed. My gratitude for the wind could so easily carry me away, were it not for the pull of my soul and soles.

The ground beneath (earth/solid), had begun to speak with me in a dialect of vibration absorbed straight through the plants of my feet. Be it sand I ran my toes through or pavement hit by the pressured land of my sneakered step, I could feel secrets to which I had not been "privy" before, run up through my body and into my consciousness. Walking, playing, even laying on the ground, made me feel more connected. It, well, grounded me. It brought my communion with nature full circle. I was being awakened - reminded that I was part of something bigger, a family of divine creations whose kinship I had forgotten to celebrate. I never wanted the adventures to end. I thought, "something else in my life is going to have to change to allow me to live these experiences more often."

After all, the timing of this epiphany was less than convenient, despite the urgency it brought with it. It was unfolding during my very busy executive management career in nonprofit and while living in my small studio apartment on the busy streets of the Bronx, New York. This was all coming up for me before my leap into self-employment. Enjoying long, nature-filled walks in that day-to-day felt rather difficult to accomplish. Instead, I took a different approach. I began to bring the four elements of nature into my home and work decor. An electric fireplace joined by a plethora of candles helped me to remember the power of fire. Scattered battery-powered fountains provided playgrounds to water. Aroma-therapy diffusers colored and scented the ever-more graceful air and I bought a money-plant at IKEA that I held as a representation of the earth. Sure, it was no walk on the beach of an island or stroll through the streets of southern Spain, like what had inspired me. It was, however, magical.

The spaces I adorned developed such a quality of light and serenity. The energy that they emanated returned such a sense of solace back to my days. In large part because of that, I was able to grow more accustomed to being in environments that induced calmness and joy, or at the very least, supported it. I loved how spa-like my home and office had become. How they served as refuge and offered me the space to think, or not think. They slowed me down and gave me perspective. It was lovely and refreshing. I had found creative ways to bring the power of nature's elements into my personal and work spaces – I decorated to inspire. And I was grateful for that. Though, deep down inside, part of me longed to commune with those elements in their most organic forms, I didn't yet know just how to pull that off permanently. So, I kept the craving at bay with short vacations every few months to new, nice places that teased my need.

That is, until I first set foot in San Diego - Winter, 2011. I was still working in nonprofit administration at the time. One of my program funders thought it imperative that I, and a few other partners from the community, attend a Federal Sustainability Conference in Southern California. Though the meetings would take place on Harbor Island, many of us were put up in quaint, cottage-style hotels up and down Coronado. I had travelled quite a bit by this point of my life (I had seen four continents, almost a dozen Caribbean islands and almost two dozen states). Travel was exciting, but I had always looked forward to returning home. Then, I landed for the first time in SoCal and felt immediately like this was home. I was inexplicably tipped off... this was not just another trip to enjoy. It was a premonition of what was to come.

Every day, I woke up to the crisp breeze of a temperate climate, shut my hotel door and walked a mile and a half to the coffee shop. One chai latte and a self-help book in hand and breakfast was complete. I could sit outside and just read for hours. It was delightful. But probably not as delightful as the walk back to the hotel. The sounds and scenes I walked through, the energy I ingested, the calm of each breath I exhaled - all somehow magical in this new place I now dreamt of calling home. I could feel every element of nature pulling me in. The sun shone down oh so strongly. Each breeze carried with it a sweet scent and calming cool. The beach's waves called from only a few feet away. It was breathtaking. I left after a week, with a strange sensation that the trip had somehow transformed my consciousness; but I couldn't, then, have told you exactly how.

What a difference a year makes. By 2012, I was feeling much better about my life. I was "doing the work," taking better care of myself, spending more and better time with myself and enjoying the greatness that it was all manifesting. I had also just begun dating this new guy - a pilot whose primary residence was San Diego, California. Interestingly enough, we had not yet met during my 2011 visit there; a fact for which I'm grateful. The time I spent alone there helped me set an intention for my life that far outlasted the trip's duration. Being by myself, with myself, helped me connect to what I loved. And doing so in sunny San Diego, helped me get clear on the kind of life I wanted to live and the kind of place that I now wanted to call home. I liked traveling, reading, writing, coaching and waking up in a place (a dwelling, a community, a geographical location) that kept me connected to nature and its four precious elements; elements with which I had begun a sacred romance that was rejuvenating my spirit.

So, I can't say that I was at all disappointed when, after three years of the healthiest relationship that I've ever experienced (now 2015), *Mr. Perfect For Me*, asked me to consider moving out west. By this point in my "wellness work," I was so much more emotionally, financially, socially, spiritually, intellectually and physically better. It was time for that dramatic occupational, and an environmental one too. I was ready to begin my consulting work, which allowed a more flexible schedule and frankly, I couldn't handle one more winter of digging my car out of New York City's snowy streets. So, I said yes - the beginning of yet another adventure whose twists and turns have been exciting and love-filled.

This morning, he and I woke up together in Anchorage, Alaska. We drove an hour to the Portage Glacier and marveled at the majesty of nature. It hit me that growing up in New York, the biggest, grandest things that I saw were made by man - buildings, bridges, even our beaches. It's almost enough to make us feel like all greatness must be man-made... Until you stand in the presence of the biggest, grandest things that God can do. Suddenly, humble and grateful become all you can feel.

We washed our faces in the natural spring water running through a roadside stream that we passed as we drove back to Anchorage. A ways further, we stopped for a hike through a natural wildlife conservation center, visited with wolves, bears and porcupines and then drove another half-hour to dinner. After dinner, we walked outdoors some more. It's Spring, so the temperature stays in the 50s and the sun stays out, beaming powerfully until about 10pm. The air is dry and soothing - comfortable at night, calming in the day.

In a week, I'll head back to New York to visit with family and friends. I'll stay in the remodeled basement apartment of my family home, where he and I now live when on the east coast. I'll write my next article for the Huffington Post, sketch at night, work out in the day, laugh a lot, love a lot and live. Ten days later, it's off to LA for a week, to shoot a few episodes for the OWN show for which I now consult (*Iyanla Fix My Life*). Then, back to meet *Mr. Perfect For Me*, at our inspirationally-decorated apartment in San Diego, CA. I'll hike and swim and coach and read and write and sketch and love every minute because for the first time in a long time, I've built a life in which I feel free.

~ Research & Wrap-Up ~

Do not underestimate the incredible healing and helping power of nature. According to Keniger, Gaston, Irvine, and Fuller (2013):

> ...there is mounting empirical evidence that interacting with nature delivers a range of measurable human benefits, including positive effects on physical health, psychological well-being, cognitive ability and social cohesion. (p.914)

Nature, however, is not the only aspect of our physical environment that can prove soothing and serene. The way that we design our space can also have a great impact on our mood. Desmet (2015) suggests that:

> ...mood can be regulated by engaging in particular activities, and these activities suggest a multitude of design opportunities: design can enable, support, and inspire people to engage in the activities that have a positive impact on mood. (p.11)

Environmental variables impacting our health and mood are surely not limited to what's contained within our walls or what of nature's elements you can access. Also important is the way we feel about the neighborhood, community and places in which we live. So, choose to live in ways and places that help you to feel free. That's one take away from a report by the Robert Wood Johnson Foundation Commission to Build a Healthier America (2008) which states that:

> Just as conditions within our homes have important implications for our health, conditions in the neighborhoods surrounding our homes can also have major health effects. Social and economic features of neighborhoods have been linked with mortality, general health status, disability, birth outcomes, chronic conditions, health behaviors and other risk factors for chronic disease, as well as with mental health, injuries, violence and other important health indicators. (p.1)

So, try enjoying nature, decorating to inspire and living in ways and places that help you to feel free. Celebrate your surroundings will help you improve your environmental wellness.

Poetic Reflection: Wellness

Who knew? How could I have known?
Who would have thought that there in the loneliness, behind
the cries and sighs and midnight, fetal position, pseudo-
psychotic lullabies, was hidden the key?...
The key to all that I had been seeking - the attention and
validation, the sweet feeling missing to silence the desperation,
the peace of magnificent creation that I had longed to be...
Who knew the key was me?
Who knew that falling in love with myself in every aspect of
who I am would have created the template the world needed
to learn how to love me properly?
Who could have seen that? Certainly not I.
For I was too blind.
Blinded by the lack of faith that allowed my demons to escape
and puppeteer the private and public parades in which my ego
chose to sashay, while I died bit by bit inside.
I hid in the shadows of my affairs with loneliness and men
Trying hard to pretend that I wasn't ready to end
This spiritual suicide
Until one day, there were just no more tears left to cry
It was time to rise
Brick by brick I rebuilt my spirit, holding every lesson tight
Honoring my emotions, feeding my intellect, treating my body
right
Paying tribute to all that surrounds me: friends, family and
natural elements alike
Celebrating abundance and pursuing my dreams until all that I
allowed to manifest was the greatness with which I was now
so aligned
And with every breath, and every test I grow more and stress
less

For I now understand the power of the journey with which
I've been blessed
Learning to fall in love with myself and moving from
loneliness to wellness!

Part III

You

❧

Fall
In Love
With Yourself

Through Our
LATINA LENS

Del Dicho Al Hecho, Hay Un Buen Trecho

My dissertation confirmed some major insights about the influence of Latinidad on our sense of self as Latinas; ones that I also found to be true in my personal experiences. Sure, there are some oppressive stereotypes that we need to revise. But overall, there are a great deal of really positive traits that are passed on to us through the use of Latino culture. Our strong work ethic, our emphasis on education and achievement, our strength and resilience, are all attributes rooted in our cultural communities.

Through those traits we find patterns of constant learning, growth, flexibility and adjustment. All of those will serve you well here. Because as you move through this, you'll find that you now have a fire in your belly that screams, "let's make a change... let's be happier... let's be healthier... let's fall in love with ourself!" But as the Spanish idiom goes, "del dicho al hecho, hay un buen trecho" (from speech to deed, there is a good stretch; or, easier said than done). It's one thing to be inspired and another to be motivated.

Understanding what we can change about ourselves is one thing. But doing the daily work can be tough. The world is full of so many distractions. School, work, family and friends can be all-consuming. And let's face it, while we are certainly not "victims," we are women of color in a society that has historically oppressed women and people of color, so there's that. Under-resourced communities and persisting wage inequality means that it feels like we're always working three times as hard to try to level the playing field. It's easy to get excited, then get exhausted. Then self-care, self-love and self-improvement quickly fall to the bottom of the priority list.

So, can we use the passion in our blood, the strength of our ancestral warriors and wisemen and the resilience and work ethic of our immigrant and migrant parents, to fuel our daily self-improvement? Can we take that focus on education

143

and learning and turn it inward? Can we, like the many generations before us, become a better version of who we've been, but with what we now know about wellness and self-care, now change our lives at light speed? Can we live a happier and healthier existence? How do we go from word to action? How do we actually make the change?...

You and Your Work

So why have I chosen to share these stories and perspectives with you? It's simple. While the details of my journey are specific to my experience, neither the path to peace that I walked nor the joy of self-love that I found, are rights reserved exclusively for me. I am certainly not unique in feeling suffocated by pain nor am I special in having been awakened by healing. As you well know, I have no monopoly on unhealthy romantic relationships and the heartbreaks they bring. More importantly, remember that I am only one of many who have gotten well after being love-sick and faithless, by building balanced and healthy habits in each of the eight dimensions of wellness that I've discussed here. That solace and serenity awaits you too. The key to unlocking it is in these three steps: work your thoughts, process your feelings and modify your behavior. I had to learn to do this in each dimension of wellness and in every aspect of my life if I was serious about learning, growing and being happy.

To do this effectively, I suggest that you begin to sort through your current thoughts, feelings and behaviors all the while making determinations about which are serving you and which are not. This will help you to let go of those that hold you back and replace them with healthier, more productive options.

9.

Develop Your
Intuitive,
Pre-Cognitive
Prophecy
(IPP)

How do you know which thoughts, feelings and behaviors serve you and which do not? Good question. You need a measuring stick. Having a standard by which to measure the usefulness of everything you think, feel and do, is integral to the process of determining which thoughts, feelings and behaviors to keep and which to replace. For this, you will need to envision the life that you wish to be living; that dream you dream; that ideal you've come to think improbable. Take a second to begin that. Think about this vision of happiness, for which you so often find yourself wishing. In some cases, it's a vision that may even have come to haunt you as you've become obsessed with your not having it. I'm familiar with that discord and understand how it tugs at you. Yet, I'm asking you now to focus on the joy it promises and the details that it holds. Remember that you're worthy of the highest gifts and that all things are possible when you align with your greatness. Let yourself imagine this life for which you long, from a place deep down in your soul. Think about how you would live were you to have no fears, no doubts and no obstacles. Stay there for a second. Close your eyes if you need to.

Now imagine that while you were reading and contemplating this, all of the issues you currently face were resolved. You look up and you are living that life that you've always dreamt of. What's different now? This is a therapeutic exercise meant to help you find solutions (Pichot & Dolan, 2003). Take some time to really feel out the answer to that question. How does it smell? Pause and allow yourself to take in what it's like to be fully present in this new reality. How does it look? What will you taste? What sounds do you hear? What's in your hands? What will you wear? Where will you go? What's on the schedule for the rest of the day? What about tomorrow? What's exciting to you now? What are you looking forward to? What are you proud of? What have you learned? What do you now carry in your soul? What have you let go of? Where do you now live? What do you now do for work? How are your relationships? What impact are you making on the world? What impact has the world made on you? What's different about the way you start your day? How do you now end your day? After each question, take a breath and consider the answer clearly as you picture it in your mind, experience it in your body and make peace with it in your heart. Think it through. Write it out.

Go as deeply with each response to each question as your imagination will take you. Don't try to solve current problems or become limited by your ideas of what's "realistic." Let yourself imagine a world in which you are truly happy and allow yourself to simply describe the manifestations of that joy. The more uncontrollably you allow yourself to go into this exercise, the truer to your spirit your revelation will be. What you are crafting here is an intuitive, pre-cognitive prophecy (IPP). This is not simply a question-and-answer exercise. It's not the making of a strategic plan or the setting of a goal. Call on your spirit to inform you. This is a light-guided, fact-finding mission, in which you collect evidence of the life you were meant to live to serve as a prediction of what's to come - a vision born into this world with you before you could think, known to your soul and attainable in your future. It is an opportunity to tap into the most divine piece of you, which knows what greatness awaits you when your spirit is aligned, and your ego has been soothed. It is your right and your gift to live your joy.

Feel the freedom of who you are in this life; the way in which things slide right off of you. Nothing can anger you because you understand every incident as simply a piece of a grander plan. You see everything as a manifestation of your consciousness, so you're open to learning what each thing is there to teach you about how you see yourself, the world and God. And you make adjustments in accordance with those lessons to live an even happier and more fulfilled life. You know that everything will work out. Thus, you're excited to see the whole picture because you know that each thing that you currently encounter is simply a minute fragment of a perfect masterpiece. But your excitement is calming. You no longer feel anxiety or impatience because you understand that those feelings are projections of a fear that something won't come, and fear comes from a lack of faith. You have faith. You don't worry. Instead, you believe! You're doing what you want. You're treated in ways that honor your spirit and you treat others in ways that honor theirs. You understand the connection - our shared, divine oneness.

You wake up grateful for what you have experienced and for the treasures that you know will continue to come. You live your days with smiles and strength and things flow because everything and everyone supports your spirit. Sure, things still happen that you didn't want. People do things that temporarily hurt your feelings. You may even feel pain, agony or discomfort in this life. But they come through your experience. They don't stay with you. They don't define you. They do not knock you off balance and they certainly do not tattoo themselves to your soul. Why? Because for this version of you, any negative reaction is temporary, worked through and released.

You keep the lesson; your consciousness expands as a result and your spirit continues to fly freely. It is unburdened by the heavy weights of the trauma you once relived with each experience that tested your faith or incident whose lesson you failed to perceive. You are a child of light. You are too busy noticing the colors of your landscape, the beauty of your neighbors and the warmth in your tummy, to get caught up in anything other than joy. You walk in the fulfillment of this prophecy. I want you to truly imagine that. Give yourself a second with closed eyes, to take a deep breath as you settle into the peace of that life, of that version of "you." Imagine that you have embraced your peace. The peace with which you came into the world. Now, as you move forward each day in the life you currently live, be mindful of every thought, feeling and behavior. If it isn't consistent with this life that awaits you and this version of you into which you are stepping, then it is not helpful and can stand to be replaced. That is your measuring stick. The IPP is your tool for determining what stays and what goes.

From this moment forward, let your IPP be the measuring stick for all that you do. Let it be the tool that you use to determine whether or not a thought, feeling or behavior is helpful. Would it be the choice of that happy, peaceful, successful you full of energy/light/God? Would you think it, feel it or act it out if you feared nothing, loved everything and moved with a sense of peace and purpose? Begin to look at your current choices in this way. Everything from what pops into your head when you first wake up, to what food gets put into your body, deserves that level of attention and evaluation.

Sure, that level of reprogramming will likely be difficult at first. In the learning of any new skill one must field through the four stages of competence (Hawkins, 2009). Initially, you stumble around through the darkness of "unconscious incompetence" (you don't know what you don't know). I wrestled with that blindness in part I of this book as I'm sure you did too during some rough patches in your past. Figuratively: you're doing the best you can to get water at night in a dark kitchen, and you keep walking into things because you can't see. After you bang yourself into enough walls, you think, "hmmm, maybe there's a light switch around here, somewhere", and you begin to crawl around in search of it.

Welcome to stage two - "conscious incompetence" (you know there are things you don't know). You start to think, "there's got to be a better way to walk around this room without constantly banging my toe into all of the baggage that I've accumulated." Just like that you come to a helpful acknowledgment - "I could get what I need without banging myself up as much if I just learned how to turn on these lights." Admitting the problem doesn't solve the problem, but it's a start. At least now you know what you need, and you begin to search for it.

That's when stage three hits - "conscious competence." You find the switch, learn how it works, and practice flicking the lights on and off. Now, you begin to walk more carefully around, not just the room, but the whole house; making sure to remember to turn on every light of every room that you enter. That is, until you reach "unconscious competence;" flicking the switch of every room that you wander into with such ease that you can do it while listening to music and texting a friend - it's just that natural.

That's the power of habit. Change can seem difficult to incorporate into your lifestyle, but the greater your commitment and the more routinely you practice it, the more it becomes a part of your fabric. You go from not knowing that life can be better, to learning how to make life better, to making life better until eventually life is so good that you're not even sure how and when you flicked on the light. You just know you did!

Now that you have your IPP in place, you have a guiding vision; but it will take change to get you there. So, stop for a second and think. Go back to that exercise in which you are the "you" of your IPP and envision how you got there. What did you do differently? What thoughts did you have to stop thinking? What feelings did you have to explore? What actions did you have to take, or behaviors did you have to cease, to embrace your true self - peaceful, positive and productive. Visualize yourself making the changes that need to take place for you to get from here to there. Then, push forward toward your IPP by changing to better reflect the "you" of that prophecy. Evaluate every choice you make and remember, nothing is neutral (Foundation for Inner Peace, 1985). It's either helping or it's hurting so challenge it all. Everything that emanates from your energy asserts to the universe your true position on who you are, what you believe you are worth and what faith you have. Analogously, every thought, feeling and behavior attracts to you the energetic equivalent of those positions. So, if it's not helpful, then it's harmful.

To put it more picturesquely, imagine yourself in the flow of a stream. The water (like divine energy) is in constant motion. Thus, if you make choices not to move forward with it, you'll be left behind. Make no mistake, moving forward does not require that you swim with the flow of the stream, although you can feel free to do so. It simply requires that you stop digging your heels into the ground to hold yourself in place. Just let go of the resistance and the river of enlightenment will carry you with it. Insist on standing still and you'll miss the bliss that awaits you. Remember, anything not moving you forward toward your IPP, is likely just holding you back. And with serenity being such a powerful stream, why dig in those heels? Why not release the resistance

(Hicks & Hicks, 2004) and enjoy the flow? Keep that image in mind as you start to sift and sort through the thoughts, feelings and behaviors in which you currently find yourself engaged. Working thoughts, processing feelings and modifying behavior are not mutually exclusive pieces of the work you are to do. Nor do they represent a liner model in which one step logically follows the other. Think of them more as the parts of an interlocking spheres of influence over your life.

10.

Work Your Thoughts

Suggestions:
Evaluate the Impact of Your Thoughts,
Examine the Root of Problematic Thoughts,
Challenge Problematic Thoughts, &
Replace Those Thoughts That Don't Serve You

If you close your eyes, take a breath and attempt to sit in silence, you'll likely find that silence is more difficult to accomplish than you may have hoped. Thanks to the incessant stream of consciousness that is constantly bombarding you, your mind has become cluttered by chaos (Tolle, 2006). Fear is hard at work reinforcing the bars of the prison it has built, while the ego frantically shackles chains around the arms and legs of our friends, faith and love. You try to quiet your mind, but you're just overwhelmed by more and more thoughts. I know that feeling well. I've been there. It's so easy to quit trying to be free of the chatter when the best parts of us are held captive by our anxiety.

A soundtrack strung together of seemingly random thoughts plays in the background, to accompany the scores of insecurities that always seem to pop up. Among them, the ongoing narratives that we have developed, practiced and perfected - narratives that paint us as unworthy and the universe as untrustworthy - narratives that we use to justify and rationalize our distrust of the world and our own personal ideas of inadequacy. We have created so many stories in our heads - stories that tell us who we are, what we're worth and what's possible. What's more, is we believe those stories, in which villains victimize us and we fail to triumph; in which life is unfair and our dreams are unrealistic. On some level, we believe in them; in their likelihood. We believe in the danger of the attacks against which we must protect ourselves. The scarcity that forces us to deprive ourselves. The cold world because of which we have lost ourselves. All the stories, these perspectives, all built on thoughts. Thoughts that we believe to their core. Thoughts that inspire our feelings and drive our behavior. Everything built on these oh, so powerful thoughts. Why, though? Why do we believe them?

It is not like our many thoughts constitute some innate representation of absolute truth, as we tend to treat them. They are not each divinely dictated bursts of insight. Few of them even possess any universal accuracy, at all. Contrary to the importance that we tend to give them, many of our thoughts, particularly those that hold us back, are in fact just social constructs – the ideas of others, that we have internalized and adopted. Sure, there are those thoughts that are divinely inspired and in-tune/intuitive. There are those that speak to our grandeur and help us to better understand the complexities of this existence. And the more aligned we become with God/the universe/source, the more of those positive thoughts we begin to have. But by far, the thoughts that get us into the most trouble are the negative ones - the ones that keep us from getting out of our own way. And those are not universally true or divinely inspired. They're just thoughts. That's why our negative thoughts need so much challenging.

Family - It begins with recognizing that many of those thoughts, that are less than helpful to your growth and development. They are messages that were embedded in you by different sectors of society (family, religion, culture, school, media, neighborhoods, etc.), who presented you with a particular perspective; one that fit their paradigm (Bronfenbrenner, 1992). Our sense of self is built on layers and layers of this information that we got from others. Think back to your early experiences as a child and you'll realize that you were born into a plethora of communal systems on which you depended for your self-image, sense of purpose and worth *(layer 1)*: your kindred, peer groups, religious families, the residents and patrons of your geographical neighborhoods, etc. You were taught how and what to think about yourself and about the things in your life, by the way that others in those groups interacted with you (Cooley, 1902): the things that were told to you, the requests made of you, the behaviors modeled for you and/or the thoughts that people and institutions encouraged from you versus those that they did not.

Community - They taught you about your value simply by the ways that they treated you, the looks that they gave you or ways that they ignored you - the symbolic place that you held. As you grew, you also began to identify yourself as part of other social groups beyond your family and friends; groups based in gender, race, class, nationality, ethnicity, sexual preference, religion, special abilities, labeled disabilities and more. And like with family, friends and neighbors, you looked to other social institutions for messages about how valuable you were and what you were meant for, given your membership to these other groups. School, the media, religious texts, your community, all constantly, in some way, sometimes unknowingly, teaching you about your power and your purpose *(layer 2)*. You took on much of what society told you about who you were as a part of these groups. And the larger that web of influences became, the more tangled in the perceptions of others your identity seemed to get; until you lost all sense of the brilliance with which you were born and the limitless potential with which you walk the earth.

Trauma - Then, as we all do, you experience some traumatic events (complex like poverty, or acute like abuse) that shatter your sense of safety, and you take it to mean that you're truly worthless and that the world really sucks *(layer 3)*. Okay, so in some ways, that's a bit of an oversimplification. But in other ways, it's pretty accurate. It's understandable too. Why wouldn't you? Although these are not necessarily universal truths about who you are and what kind of world you live in, they are quite easy to believe given what you've experienced. After all, when you are overwhelmed by pain, it is easy to see the trauma of your reality in those sad moments as representing the sum total of the universe's possibilities.

Romance - Then years pass, and you likely experiment with other relationships, some of which further test and devalue your sense of self *(layer 4)*. Two wounded people, coming together to do emotional work that they've been avoiding, serving as mirrors for one another in these "special relationships" (Williamson, 1992) where your biggest challenges lie, a mere reflection of your own issues. Let's be honest, if you haven't learned how to work your thoughts, that's just what your romantic relationships are like. So, they hurt. Which only serves to further perpetuate your story about how you'll never find happiness and how much fun the universe is probably having at your expense: God in a mythical cloud, laughing at your sadness, using your pain for his/her own amusement.

By this point, you've pretty much lost sight of the light that's being covered up by all the *layers* of soot you've accumulated throughout the years (Williamson, 1992). How could you not? With each relationship and each experience came a story that taught you something, true or not, about you, the world and God. This is how unimportant you are, because look how little time your parents were willing to spend with you. This is all you can accomplish as a brown person. This world's dangerous for women. Hard work is the key, blind faith is for the lazy. Dreamers never prosper.

There's not enough of anything. Don't trust people. Be a "real" man. Be practical. Don't be selfish. The list goes on.

It may sound silly when ranted off that way but make no mistake - we believe the lies: that we're not good enough, that we are not safe, that we don't matter, that we can't change, that we will never reach that goal, that we're better off just settling, that we were born to suffer. It's all the makings of a real-life sleeper-cell agent. We come across one word, symbol or circumstance, and we're triggered. The stories start to play, and we become aggressive, defeated, dangerous and self-destructive all in the name of some cause/thought (the story) to which we don't even remember pledging our loyalty. We get lost in thoughts that are not even our own, many of which are not at all true, and let them rip us apart from the depths of our core.

Sound familiar? That's because it has likely happened to you. People convinced you of what they thought was true. So, what you learned was not the truth about who you really are and what you can truly do. Instead, what you learned were ways of thinking that helped you to navigate those many social systems full of other people and their ideas. In that way, they may have helped you to get through what you had to get through. For that, be grateful! But what you learn to help you get through something won't necessarily help you to get out of it. The same tools that helped you survive those systems, can also keep you from thriving. That locked door that kept you safe, could also keep you trapped. Ways of thinking that may have once helped you, can sometimes keep you stuck - attracting the same energy you complain about, which only validates your belief in the stories that you tell yourself. Those thoughts can become their own self-fulfilling prophecy, helping you to only focus your attention on any evidence in the world that supports their seeming truth. Your vision becomes selective, open to seeing only what confirms the "validity" of your existing thoughts (Nickerson, 1998). And to be clear, whatever you seek, so you shall find. If your thoughts guide you to good, there you will make a home. Should your thoughts guide you to fear, so too will you find a place there.

That is why you must work your thoughts: evaluate their impact, examine their roots, challenge them, and replace those that don't serve you. Remember that the mere fact that you have a thought does not make it true, trustworthy or helpful to you in building a better life. At best, you learned to think some of those thoughts to help you navigate the life you've been living which means that their usefulness is limited in scope. They may or may not be useful to you moving forward, depending on what pieces of your life you are allowing to change. At worst, they are keeping you stagnant, preventing you from finding peace. Basically, while many of them are great, some are useless, and others are dangerous. Thus, they must be challenged.

Again, remember that having a thought, does not make it true. And focusing on a time when a particular thought may have been true, does not necessarily make it helpful. Remember that your thoughts must be helpful to your growth if you are to move into the greatest version of you. That's why you must learn to work your thoughts if you truly want to grow. To do so, take the following steps: Evaluate their impact, Examine their roots, Challenge them and Replace those that don't serve you.

Evaluate the Impact of Your Thoughts

When you think a thought, listen to your body instead of to your mind as the thought unfolds. How does it feel to think that thought on a scale from 0 (low energy) to 10 (high energy)? Is your energy higher or lower because of this thinking? Do you feel better about yourself or worse? Is it aligned with your IPP - is it aligned with the best version of who you are? Is it a thought that promotes a sense of peace and calm or a thought that fills you with anger and anxiety? That is the most helpful way to analyze the usefulness of your thought patterns – do they make you tense or set you free? What impact does the thought have on your body? Do your shoulders drop as you think it or does your entire frame contract? Do you breathe through the thought or hold your breath while you think it? Is it a memory that makes you smile or one that makes you scared?

When you experience a thought, stop and take a second to weigh the impact of what you are thinking. I'm not being heard. I'm misunderstood. I won't be taken care of. My needs won't be met. I can't trust her/him. There won't be enough for me. I will not be safe. I'm not important. I'm not valued. I'm not worth it. It's not possible. Good stuff never happens to me. I'm not lucky like that. These are the types of problematic thoughts that poison your body and your spirit when you let them live in your mind. Take a second to become aware of what thoughts you are thinking each moment of each day and consider what impact they are having on you, your health, happiness and overall wellness.

Examine the Root of Problematic Thoughts

Once you have evaluated the impact of a thought and found it to be problematic, take a second to think about how that thought came to be part of your way of thinking. Though it is not necessary to trace the genesis of every thought, it can be helpful. It is, sometimes, very enlightening to consider the sources of what we treat as wisdom. Sometimes it's the 6th grade bully that called us ugly or the well-meaning advice of our slightly paranoid loved one. Whether the thought came from a relative trying to protect you or a person whose pain inspired them to hurt you, one thing holds true – just because they said it or believed it does not make it true or helpful to you. Begin to understand these thoughts as the confused ramblings of wounded, imperfect individuals who, despite their intentions, are fallible and did the best that they could for what they knew and who they were. This will increase your ability to distance these thoughts from your identity.

Seeing them as the ideas of others will help make it easier to challenge them. It will help you separate from them, to let go of seeing them as absolute truths planted inside you by some all-knowing power and allow you to see them for what they truly are, other people's opinions that you have taken on; ideas that have been established by social forces interested in controlling you (even if only to protect you). While they may have helped you in some way to navigate the world in which you live, these cognitive constructs upon which you have built your sense of self, your beliefs about the world, your feelings about God/source energy, are not absolute truths. They are theories that were posed to you, which you often believed because you somehow trusted the theorist. It was a loved one, a social institution, a person you admired, the media you thought represented you, the family who vowed to protect you or a teacher whose knowledge you were encouraged to let guide you.

Their intentions may have been honorable, their opinions may have been useful to them in navigating their world, in their way; and their ideas may have been wise in their place and in their time. That does not, however, mean that those thoughts will be helpful to you in your wellness evolution. Consider from where each of those problematic thoughts may have come. Examining the root of a thought will likely prove helpful to you in understanding why and how you came to believe it the way that you do and that will help you to begin letting go of the power that you have given it.

Challenge Problematic Thoughts

Once you have examined the roots of your problematic thinking and debunked the power they used to carry as make-believe truths, you can now begin to challenge them. Are they true, always and everywhere? Are they trustworthy? Are they helpful? Who, when and where are the exceptions to these ideas? Begin to make lists, in your mind, or on paper, of people and events not consistent with these thoughts. Consider what you may not be considering. For instance, if the thought is that you are never heard, as we explored in the last section, consider the following: what if you are being heard and it is just difficult for others to demonstrate it? When have you been understood and what made that possible? What are the many life events in which you have been taken care of? Which of your many needs have been met? Begin to collect the proof needed to disprove these thoughts. If they are not helpful, then they are not true to your spirit, and all that it takes to begin challenging them, is your willingness to find the evidence of their dishonesty.

Remember, these stories that we tell ourselves, these narratives that we build – they all have flip-sides and exceptions that will serve you in challenging the thought that bred the story. They will help you in challenging the thoughts that feed the story and they will begin to alter the filter through which you perceive the world. The more that you challenge the thoughts that you have allowed to shape your views, the greater your paradigm shift will be. Take inventory of the things that have gone well, worked out, redefined what was possible and affirmed your value. Look at your life and to the experiences of others, for if it can happen for them, it can happen for you. Focus on what will help you to be happier, healthier and more productive: refuse to believe in anything that fosters doubt in your past, present or future greatness.

Replace Those Thoughts That Don't Serve You

Once you have challenged the validity and usefulness of your problematic thoughts, it is helpful to start replacing them with more helpful thoughts. For this, you want to think of ideas, opinions and statements that speak to the truth of who you are and the greatness of possibilities in which you exist. This is when affirmations are best posed to work because you have done the work necessary to clear a way for them. You have made room for them to take hold by lessening any internal resistance you may have had to their message. Now, you can see in yourself more of what they are meant to show you.

The best way to use affirmations is to make them as general as possible and ensure that they are built around something positive that you truly believe to your core; something you have no resistance around, or the least resistance around (Hicks, 2004). Find one of those exceptions or flipsides and look for the truth in what they teach you. Then, create a statement around the truth that also affirms your worth: "I am well taken care of, I am worth taking the time to get to know, I am talented, I am unique in my value to the world, I am trustworthy, I am trusting, I can heal." As you replace the limiting thoughts with more helpful ones, make sure you call to mind examples of when these thoughts have been true to serve as evidence of their validity and to give them power. They need the strength to conquer those less-than-helpful thoughts that you have spent so much time believing.

11.

Process Your Feelings

Suggestions:
Be Aware of Your Feelings,
Explore Your Feelings,
Sit with Your Feelings, &
Let the Harmful Feelings Go

Feelings and emotions are terms often used interchangeably. We, too, will likely progress to using them that way here. Research, however, has made many distinctions between the two words. One such distinction is worth noting as part of our discussion: there are those who suggest that feelings are experienced internally, while emotions are expressed externally (Fortin, Dwamena, Frankel, & Smith, 2012). According to this model, feelings include experiences of abandonment, bliss, confusion, etc. The word "emotions," on the other hand, is a term technically used to describe the expressions of those feelings. That encompasses reactions like anger and excitement that are often noticeable in a person. It may seem like semantics to get caught up in these demarcations, so we won't for long. I only bring it up because it is helpful to our learning, to think of feelings and emotions as layered one on top of the other. They build on one another, turning an initial internal reaction into a complex set of behaviors. To further complicate the use of these similar and overlapping terms, we might also consider the role of "mood." Your mood is an emotional state of being, an attitude or tone that, for a short while, dominates your person. It does not revolve around an event, but instead colors your general character in a moment because of feelings you may have experienced in the past. You'll notice that your feelings will often lead to emotions that then create moods. Keep an eye on that set of reactions. Your awareness of it is important to your healing. However, what we are most concerned with here, is learning how to deal with the feelings that come up for you. So, let's walk through that a bit.

Per the Modal model (Gross, 2007), there are four pieces to the feelings puzzle: 1. A situation (real or imagined); 2. Your attention to that situation (focusing on it brings it into your consciousness); 3. Your appraisal of the situation (do you interpret it as negative or positive and why); and 4. Your response to that interpretation which causes an internal change in experience (in your mind, body and spirit).

As you can see, the way that you think about things plays a key role in the way that you feel. That's why it's so important that we work our thoughts; because our thoughts, our beliefs, those intense stories that we tell ourselves are crucial to this. They determine the situations to which we pay attention. They color the filter through which we interpret and appraise the situations we encounter. They also tell us how to respond to those interpretations. Our thoughts are intricately enmeshed with our feelings. I used to believe, like many, that my thoughts and my feelings were largely unrelated. Perhaps they coexisted, but one had little to do with the other. It was a shock to me to learn that everything that I believed to be feeling in my heart, was a result of something that I had chosen to continue believing in my mind. That's the beauty of it, you can choose to feel differently by making a choice to think about a situation differently. However, this is impossible to do if you don't understand the feelings that you are having, the ways that they affect you and the alternatives available to you. That is why it is so important that you process them. Particularly, the negative ones.

All sorts of research has been conducted and theories developed to help us do just that. There are countless works in emotional intelligence (Goleman, 1995) and emotional literacy (Steiner, 2003), emotion management and emotion regulation (Vingerhoets, Nyklíček & Denollet, 2008) - all giving us the ins and outs of what we feel, why we feel and what to do about it. Everyone calls it something different and each label has its own unique articulation of the key factors involved. Still, the premise underlying all of them is consistent. We can easily become consumed by our negative emotional reactions to the situations in our lives and if we don't learn to take control of those reactions, they will begin to control us. They will create relationships, take jobs, walk away from opportunities, jeopardize healthy interactions and otherwise sabotage our joy, all the while representing a very small part of who we truly are and yet creating a big mess. That's what unprocessed negative emotions tend to do. They take a small reaction to a seemingly upsetting incident that could be short-lived and turn it into an attitude toward the world, a mood you can't shake or sometimes a consequence you fix.

We all know folks who are easily affected by negative feelings. In fact, we've all had moments when the same could be said of us. Something happens that we perceive as unfair or unjust. We feel hopeless and unsafe and we become angry or sad. It feels as though heat is building up around the base of our hearts as it tightens, becoming more and more tense. Our ability to reason starts to fade, our amygdala starts to reign and suddenly, we're thinking more about how to protect ourselves than we are about how to progress within ourselves. We become more concerned with defending ourselves against a situation that we have now interpreted as a threat, than we are with taking the opportunity to elevate beyond it.

I've done it so many times. My guess is that you have as well, for there are very few of us who can claim never to have had that experience. It's so very easy to do. The ego, the part of us that is deeply connected to this existence (to this body, to this place and time) is often profoundly disconnected from truth (the grandeur of spirit, the expansiveness of space, the boundlessness of time). Its job is to help us believe the myth of individualism, the illusion of separation, so that we can more independently experience the world. In this way, we can learn to better know what we are, by believing that there is something we are not. The ego's function is to keep us mindful of the contrast.

When you believe that your feelings are hurt, ask yourself whether it is your spirit or your ego that was injured by the situation. Did you feel disrespected, misunderstood, unheard, disregarded, neglected or cheated? If so, you're likely working from ego. You're responding from a place of condition (Hicks, 2004), afraid that your work will double, or your lover will leave; uncertain of how to get your needs met. These are reasonable experiences, but if they go unprocessed, they are likely to result in unhelpful reactions. You can tell your ego responses apart from your spirit responses through one clear criteria. Ego responses are sponsored by fear; spirit responses are sponsored by love. Thus, ego responses are motivated by stories of scarcity, while spirit responses are motivated by beliefs in abundance. Ego responses are based in myths of separation while spirit responses are sourced in an understanding that we are all one. Ego responses rely on your desire for control, while responses of the spirit feed on your faith. Ego responses create tension. Spirit responses inspire a sense of calm. Your ego leads with fight or flight. Your spirit leads with "I'm alright!"

This is not to suggest that you cannot trust your feelings. On the contrary. Your true feelings are very reliable. They carry an energetic power that is very much aligned with source energy and the light of who you are. They inspire your intuition and help guide you toward people and experiences that further your growth. I am not suggesting that you cease honoring your feelings. I am instead, asking that you begin listening to them, exploring those that are negative, challenging and releasing them, so that you may dig deep enough through them, sorting them all out, to find the spirit-sponsored ones that most resonate with the greatest version of you. I'm asking you to make more deliberate decisions around what you choose to feel, for how long and with what intensity, so that you can begin to let go of the feelings that don't serve you, to make space for those that do. I'm advising you to learn the process of processing your feelings and emotions. For I truly believe that in learning to do so, you will discover pieces of who you are that you have long ignored. You will face pieces of your past that you have run from and suppressed. You will gain an appreciation for the life situations in which you currently find yourself and you will lay the groundwork for the many growth opportunities promised by your future.

Whether we're talking about developing emotional intelligence, learning to be emotionally literate or learning to manage and/or regulate the many emotional responses that you may have, there are certain skills that always come up. It's important to be able to identify your feelings and emotions - know what you're feeling and what caused it. It's important to understand what thoughts are tied to those feelings and emotions and to be able to change your thoughts about an experience. It's important to understand the impact that a feeling may have on you and the power it has in the moment. It's also imperative that you find ways to relieve the intensity of the feeling, release it and repair the place it used to take up.

In short, the process of processing your feelings require you to be aware of your feelings, explore your feelings, sit with your feelings and let the harmful ones go.

Be Aware of Your Feelings

How often does a situation trigger a feeling within us, without us even realizing it? We've become so numb to the bombardment of stimuli that defines our everyday, that we're not in tune with our bodies or our psyches throughout most of our interactions. It makes sense really. If we were to stop each time we felt something and give ourselves a few hours to process what we were feeling, we would likely get very little done. So, we suck it up and keep it moving. Over time, we become so good at sucking it up and keeping it moving that we lose our ability to connect with what we're really feeling at any given moment. Call it a coping mechanism, an occupational hazard, adulthood, whatever. The truth is that we begin to look at feelings as inefficient weaknesses reserved for needy people with the luxury of time on their hands.

While it is true that you cannot deconstruct every emotional response to every situation, you should certainly put some time and energy into processing the strong ones. That is why developing an awareness of what you're feeling is so very important. As soon as you experience a disruption to your harmony, you have entered a feeling state. It could be positive, or it could be negative. Remember, a strong negative reaction is a departure from the greatness within you. That makes it worth processing: Do you feel energetic or do you feel drained? Scan your body for a sense of tightness or one of relaxation. Something has changed within you. What is it? Are you less connected to source or more connected to source? Do you feel at peace or in danger? Is your instinct to protect yourself or to rest in the feeling that all is well? Is your immediate internal reaction to try to control the situation or to have faith that all things are conspiring in your favor? Are you being led by ego or are you being led by spirit? Where on the spectrum from 0 (maximum ego influence) to 10 (maximum spirit influence) would this feeling lie?

Explore Your Feelings

Once you have built an awareness of this feeling, it's time to explore it some. Now that you know that you're having a strong negative reaction, ask yourself, "just what am I reacting to?" What do you perceive as the threat? What fear is being triggered for you? This is often very difficult to deconstruct because fear lives in layers. Like an onion, you must peel away at the layers of fear to reach the root around which it's built. When you find yourself feeling something, identify what you believe it to be. But don't stop there. It is not enough to think you know what you're feeling. Ask yourself, "why am I feeling that way?" Look for the story that's producing the feeling and then go to that feeling. Then ask yourself again, "so why am I feeling that?" It can seem tedious but there is no doubt that the treasure is worth the digging.

Angry? What's under that anger? What are you angry about? You're angry that people don't listen to you? How does that make you feel? Unheard? Does that make you feel like you're not worth listening to? And does that make you feel unworthy? Unworthy of what? Unworthy of being heard? And then, if you're not worthy of being heard, are you possibly not seen as valuable, not worthy of being respected or not worthy of being loved? And if you are unlovable then how will you ever find someone to stay with you? What if you can't? What if they don't? Will you end up alone? In this case, what gets triggered is the fear that you'll end up alone. This is just one example of going deep into a fear, and we can go even deeper into why you're afraid of ending up alone, but you get the point. For a situation to evoke a strong negative emotional reaction from you, it must have triggered a deep-rooted profound fear. The only way to explore the fear behind the feeling, behind the feeling, behind the feeling, behind what you think you might be feeling, is to peel back the layers and ask the tough questions. What are you really feeling when you think you're feeling what you think you're feeling? What's the fear?

Sit with Your Feelings

Once you've dug deep into what it is that you might be feeling, it's time to sit with the discomfort of your feelings. Acknowledgement of that root fear will usually come with memories of other times you felt this fear, things in your life that perpetuate this fear and the intense sadness and anger that comes with feeling any fear at all. Let yourself sit in the fear. Whether it means excusing yourself from a meeting for a quick bathroom break or asking your lover for an hour or two before you all continue this discussion, you deserve some time to sit in the emotion that you're feeling. And you need that time. Suppressing it too easily will only cause it to pop back up unsolicited, later. Addressing it too quickly will cause you to react from a place of discomfort and pain. Don't run from it. Don't run to it. Don't run at all. Just sit.

You've likely become so afraid of letting yourself feel this fear, and feel this pain, that you've made all kinds of decisions to avoid it; decisions that are not aligned with the best version of you. If that's true, then fear of facing the fear has come to control you. You need to live with knowing that facing this fear and sitting with this pain and discomfort will not kill you. And the only way to do that is to live through "the sitting" with it. So, sit with it. Cry if you must. Scream if you must. Breathe through the palpitations. Hold yourself if it's soothing. Sigh if it helps. Let the feeling of fear overwhelm you. Feel the uncertainty. Feel the pain. Experience every second of anxiety and insecurity, of unhappiness and angst, of strong negative emotion. Don't judge yourself for anything you feel, for you have the right to your feelings. Don't scold yourself for anything you remember. Don't lecture yourself about any future events that you feel tempted to try to predict. Just feel.

Let the Harmful Feelings Go

Now that you've let the feeling run its course, it's time to begin moving forward. Dealing with your feelings is easier once you've become aware of them, explored them and sat with them a bit. Now, it is time to get out of those feelings. Let them go. There are several ways to release yourself from the grip of these strong negative emotional reactions. These suggestions are, by far, not mutually exclusive, nor is this list exhaustive. Still, what follows are a few ways for you to begin letting go of feelings and emotions that do not serve you.

Meditate - Engage in the visualization of a moment in which the problem has been resolved. Feel the calm that awaits you. Remind yourself that this situation and the residual energy of your strong negative emotional reaction are both temporary. Try to quiet your mind, clearing it of all thoughts and begin releasing the feelings in your body, mind and spirit.

Pray - Ask a higher power for help. Whether you believe that higher power to be God or the part of your psyche that's wiser than what you are feeling right now. There is always something greater to connect to. Tap into it.

Journal - Write every word of how you're feeling, raw and uncomfortable as it may be. Then make a list of things that are going well in your life and things for which you are grateful.

Communicate - Think about the situation that caused the reaction. What calm way can you go about addressing it? Who do you need to communicate with? How do you compassionately validate what the other person needs? How do you respectfully, yet assertively advocate for what you need (now that you have a better sense of what that really is)? What can you work to change?

Distract yourself - Listen to relaxing music, crochet, eat your favorite sweets, read a book and/or light some incense or scented candles that make it easy to get lost in the smell. Use your senses to help distract you from the issue at hand. You don't want to avoid a problem or run away, but you do want to change your energy before you confront it and sometimes, time itself helps to ease the matter.

12.

Modify Your Behavior

Suggestions:
Set Goals,
Prompt Yourself to Do Better,
Reward Yourself, &
Enjoy the Manifestation

I f you're serious about being more successful, happier and healthier, then you'll have to modify your behavior in each of the eight dimensions of wellness: Emotionally, financially, spiritually, socially, in your occupation, physical habits, with your intellect and environment. Remember, you have thoughts and feelings around each dimension of wellness that keep you stuck where you are. Financial - what are the stories that you tell yourself and the feelings you experience around bills and other expenses? Social - what are the thoughts and feelings that come up for you when you need to ask for help or create boundaries with people? Physical - why haven't you gotten on that treadmill or made it to that yoga class? And so on, and so on. You'll have to do things differently than you've been doing them to create experiences different from those you've been living. Change is simple, yet quite difficult all at the same time.

It is often made easier by understanding why you've become used to living the way you have - why you've made certain choices and continue to see things in certain ways. That's where working your thoughts and processing your feelings come in handy. Those steps help you get at some of the narrative that has been shaping your story thus far. And as you look toward growth in each wellness dimension, understanding why you do what you do can help you bridge that gap between who you are and who you're striving to become. By working your thoughts and processing your feelings, you challenge the source of those choices that aren't serving you and create a space to do better now that you know better. You make it easier for yourself. Now that you've learned how to work some of those thoughts and process some of those feelings, it's time to engage in techniques that will help modify your current behavior. It is time to engage in more productive, healthy, happy lifestyle habits.

Ask yourself, what do I want to change and why? Now, we are talking about action. What do you want to do differently? What do you want to do more of? What would you like to do less of? This is the time to spring into action and make some changes. Per the Transtheoretical Model of Behavior Change, there are six stages of change: pre-contemplation, contemplation, preparation, action, maintenance and termination (Shumaker, Ockene & Riekert, 2008).

Pre-contemplation is the first stage. Some describe this as the "not ready" stage, or the stage when people are just plain old not interested in changing. You either don't think it's necessary to make any changes or you've tried, failed and become convinced that changing is just not possible. I like to think of this stage as the "I'm good" stage. People might give you feedback and suggest you make changes, but your overall attitude is, "nah, I'm good!" And in your mind, you are. You're IPP-less. You haven't tasted the sweetness of being in tune with your IPP and thus, you're willing to stay in whatever you're currently living. My guess is that if you've been called to this book, and made it this far through the pages, then you've likely already evolved beyond this stage.

The second stage is contemplation. At this point, you can pretty much recite the pros and cons of changing, right off the top of your head. You've weighed the consequences and understand the benefits that you would gain if you listened better, shopped less, meditated more, partied less, pursued your dreams, worked out more, tried some new things or spent some time in nature (whatever your goal is – insert here). You're also astutely aware of the arguments you would "lose," attention you might not get, the time you could use for other things, the loneliness you would face, the pay cut you might have to take, the ache you might feel and the fear and anxiety you'd experience. And that back and forth creates a feeling of ambiguity that makes it hard to act. I like to call this the, "I know, I know" stage. People might give you feedback and suggest you make changes, and your response, verbal or nonverbal, is "I know, I know!" And you do know, somewhere deep in your spirit; but it has yet to translate to your consciousness, or to something tangible that can be seen. I'm guessing you've passed this stage too.

Next is preparation. Here you're doing the research and taking some preliminary steps toward living differently. You've consulted someone, bought a book, joined a club - done something that demonstrates your interest in being different. You're serious about wanting to change, and motivated to do so, but you're not necessarily 100% committed yet. You're testing the waters a bit. I like to call this the "I'm working on it stage." You're not really working on it yet, but you're close enough. So, when people come to you with some feedback about what you may want to do differently, your initial response, verbal or non-verbal is, "I'm working on it."

Then there's action. This means an observable difference in the way you do things. In my world, it's you more closely aligning with your IPP. It's behaving in a way that more profoundly resonates with your IPP. It's a demonstration, in the way that you think, feel and behave, that you recognize the greatness of which you are made and of which you are a part. It's an active, constant engagement in loving yourself in each dimension of wellness. It's an honoring of all that you are and all that you bring. I like to call this the "Let's do this" stage. In this stage your energy is up and you're excited about doing things in a healthier way. It's still a struggle sometimes. You still feel tempted to skip that workshop and go get ice cream or think that thought that you know keeps you stuck, but it's becoming easier and easier to stick with this new way of life.

In the maintenance stage, you feel even less tempted to return to your old ways. You're enjoying the pay-off from the work you've done and the changes you've made. You feel good and while you might still sometimes struggle to get up and go do what's important, those struggles are few and far between. You feel much more in control. That's why I like to call this the, "I got this" stage. When you're presented with a situation that may have been challenging in the past, you now think to yourself, "I got this."

Termination is the last stage of this model. It's better referred to as "completion." I like to call it the "I woke up like this" stage (song reference, thank you Beyoncé). At this point, the change has been so well incorporated into your daily way of life, that you're never tempted to go back to who you used to be. Every day you wake up ready to face the world with your new attitude, new skills and new way of being.

For many of us, our journey through these six stages is less of a linear process and much more of a zig-zaggy line that sometimes forms circles midway. Whether it was me learning how to have healthier romantic relationships or just no longer consuming alcohol, the growth was less of a steady graduation from one stage to the other and much more of a dynamic curly line that brought me back and forth between contemplation and maintenance with stops to everything in between. The same may also be true for you. If so, there are few things that work to help push you from one stage to the other. The greatest motivators are the intrinsic ones - those things within us that move us - our values, beliefs, sense of purpose, feelings of fulfillment, joy and IPP (Intuitive, Precognitive, Process). What is it that drives you? What made you pick up this book? What makes you want to think differently, feel differently, act differently and thus live differently? What do you enjoy and how can you use it to help facilitate the change (like me watching "The Good Wife" on the treadmill)? What ignites and satisfies your curiosity? What can you do to feel more competent and confident in your ability to make these changes? What do you need to learn? Who do you need to talk to?

Making significant changes to your behavior will take time and can be difficult in some ways. To help keep you on track, try the following tips:

Set Goals

You've developed your IPP to help guide you through change and that vision will prove most useful. But it's also helpful to develop smaller goals that you can use as stepping stones toward the life of your IPP. To help you do this in a simple way, you may want to use the SMART model (Human Kinetics, 2010). Your goals should be specific (S), measurable (M), achievable or assignable (A), realistic (R), and time-sensitive (T).

Don't simply say, "I'm going to improve my emotional wellness." Be specific as to how you will do it. Make a choice to engage in a particular activity, such as meditation. Also, make a commitment that you can measure. Commit to starting off by meditating twice per week, for 20 minutes each time, or whatever you believe is feasible to start. You want to avoid setting a goal that is too difficult at first because trying and not reaching it may deter you from trying again. Instead, go for something challenging but achievable. Don't set a goal to begin meditating for hours on the mountains of Nepal if you live in Brooklyn and don't have a passport. Sure, you can work toward the time in Nepal, but start with a seat on a blanket on the floor beside your bed, in the morning when you wake. And be realistic. If you know that your mornings are busy, plan to introduce it at night once everyone has gone to sleep. Another key factor is developing a timeline. Commit to making this change within a certain time and to dedicating a certain amount of time into growing in that area. Even if you start next week with just 40 minutes, it's good to give yourself a timeline to hold to.

Prompt Yourself to Do Better

A good way to stay on track is to set up "prompts" that encourage you to engage in the healthier behavior that you're now trying to adopt. Those prompts can take several forms. Set up reminders on your phone that alert you at a particular time of day, with text suggesting what you can do to move along the change. Have an accountability partner who will call you to keep you motivated and accompany you to a meeting, a class, a workshop or just take part in a discussion with you about your progress with the change. Make the healthier option easily available to you. If you're trying to improve your eating habits, fill your fridge with only healthy options. If you're trying to work out more, put the treadmill by the bed so you bump into it all the time.

Writing positive affirmations on cards, that you place around your house, is another helpful way to provoke new ways of thinking. Again, they must be based on things you actually believe, on some level, that you can achieve. You certainly can find positive things to post. A quote from someone you know, who said something nice about you. An accomplishment you feel proud of, that you can sum up in a few words. Your favorite page of a book you read that resonated with you at your core and felt inspirational to your spirit. These are all worthy things to have around your home, or your office, to bring your consciousness back to what you want to be thinking about. Images also work. Post pictures of you at your best. Surround yourself with photos of that favorite vacation, that flattering outfit, that family that keeps you focused on being a better person. Build a vision board if it works for you and collage together the very many details of your IPP.

Reward Yourself

One very good reason to set SMART goals is to make it easy for you to track your progress, that way you create short-term wins for which you can constantly reward yourself. Creating short-term wins for yourself keeps your momentum strong and rewards keep the process of change fun. Say that your goal is to work out more. One of the negative associations that your mind might make to the thought of working out, is feeling sore. So, what about scheduling yourself a monthly trip to the spa; that way you not only have a great day to reward yourself for your hard work, but you also give yourself something fun to look toward. Similarly, if your goal is to make it to a meeting, a class or a workshop, think of setting up a "FroYo" date with a good friend right after. Of course, it doesn't have to be frozen yogurt. Think of what you like. What do you enjoy? What do you value? Use your existing healthy interests to help motivate you around the changes that you're making. Leverage what you like to help move you closer to what you want.

If you're looking to grow in your romantic relationships, take a deep breath when you walk away from that toxic romance or when you make a choice not to pick a fight in the good one. Then think about what you can do to soothe yourself and reward yourself for the efforts you've made. Sometimes a nice vacation alone is just what you need. Other

times, you may look to do something quicker, easier, cheaper
and more low key. Try writing a thank you card to yourself.
Praise yourself for the great life you'll live because of the
healthy choices you're making now.

Enjoy the Manifestation

Manifesting what you want is a process. Like most other
processes, it can take time. Remember, you've spent decades
becoming the person that you currently are, and change isn't
going to happen overnight. But change will certainly come.
So, don't be so fixated on the goals, the vision or the IPP for
that matter, that you become incapable of living life well right
now. We are all works in progress. Do the work. Watch the
progress. It is a journey. Some days will be easy, others
manageable and still others tough. But ultimately, you will get
there, and when you arrive, you will see farther now and set
your sights on new horizons once more. Get comfortable with
change as a process.

Don't look for every change to happen quickly or get stuck
in needing others to validate your change for it to feel
worthwhile. Don't judge yourself if you relapse and add that
relapse to the story you tell yourself about how you'll never be
different, and you'll never do more. Don't look for ways to
numb any discomfort you might feel while going through the
change or let the feeling of discomfort punk you out of
changing altogether. Enjoy the change. Enjoy the uncertainty
of what tomorrow will bring and the certainty that you can
handle it. Align with the fact that you are perfect, here and
now, but that every minute will be better as you get closer and
closer to the you of your IPP and strengthen the alliance
between your existence and your spirit. Delight in the
progress you make each day that your thoughts, feelings and
behavior become a greater and greater reflection of the
greatness you carry. Push yourself, challenge yourself and feel
the burn in each dimension of wellness as you become

healthier and happier than you were yesterday. Embrace your ups and downs, your big wins and small wins, your supporters and your doubters, your entire journey. Love the ride.

The truth is that working your thoughts and processing your feelings is the real heavy lifting. If you do that, behavior modification goes from being something you must work hard to do, to being a logical byproduct of your new alignment.

Some More About You...

L et's continue with the IPP imagery here to paint a helpful picture. Imagine that within you, under the language your brain adopted and behind the feelings you use to react to your social world, there is and has always been a glow. A glow that illuminates the path you are meant to travel, that reenergizes the physical vehicle you occupy and that projects for you an image of what's 10-20 miles ahead. Now imagine that your greatest, purest desires are not actually desires at all, but merely these projections of what awaits you; not images of a destination or a wish but foreshadowing of milestones that will highlight your progress. That's what your IPP is - a preview.

Imagine that you've been granted a preview to keep you focused on your path - not to torture you in the time that it takes to manifest, but to give a clue of what's coming. And imagine that it was guaranteed to be there, whether it took you 20 minutes or 20 lifetimes to walk that path. Could you enjoy the walk? Could you remember that the trees and ponds that you pass on the way are as beautiful as the projection toward which you journey? Could you drink from those ponds and eat from those trees and allow the journey to sustain you? Could you marvel at the beauty of the friends met along the way and shower in the rainstorms that surprised you? Could you play with what animals showed up and sleep serenely in beds made of dreams and stones? Could you release the vision in order to enjoy the present? Could you let the prophecy guide you without distracting you from the lessons that the journey presents? Could you let the prophecy guide you without you being tortured by its distance from you? Could you get lost in the beauty and balance of the path, knowing that you will get there?

My guess is that you could. You could, if you truly believed it would be there waiting for you, no matter what; if you felt safe on that journey. You could if you felt deep within your soul that it was guaranteed. If you held to the truth that you deserve it and can have it because you are worthy, and it is possible. And if you knew that even that bliss of which you dream, that big dream that you described as your IPP, isn't even the end-all-be-all of the goodness that awaits you. It's just the next of many great things to come when you align your spirit with greatness. Like signs on a highway, these projections are simply ways to let you know that there's a rest stop up ahead.

Don't be misled by the beauty of the projection. No matter how pretty it looks, it's not the destination. It's simply a chance to rest your longing. Once you get what you've been wanting, you're likely to begin wanting something more. Which is perfect, because life has so much more to give you. The beautiful rest stops never stop. Neither does the journey. There are so very many beautiful stops on this endless spiritual road trip, with beautiful views and cute little shops. And each time you arrive at a stop, you rest to prepare for the journey to come.

Here's a note though: your soul is always in tune with the joy for which you are meant and the many ways in which it can and will manifest. And, there's always more good to come. But there's also plenty of good around you today and inside of you always. So, there's no use living your life always waiting for the conditions of that IPP to manifest in order for you to be the "you" of that IPP - happy and healthy. You can choose to be that "you" now.

How often do you think, feel, say and behave as, "if I just had that job I've been wanting, then I could relax?" "If I had money, I would travel." "When the kids are older, I'll focus more on myself." When I retire, I'll do the things that I truly enjoy." "If people treated me more respectfully, I would calm down." "When he changes, I'll be happy." Those are all conditions that you've placed on your joy. They are usually not even part of your purest desires and thus, not even IPP-factors or glow projections. They're just limitations that you've placed on your freedom to choose happiness. Let the "you" who you think you would be if that prophecy was fulfilled, be the "you" of every day. You don't have to put those if/when conditions on it. At any given moment, you can choose to be the "you" of your IPP.

The "you" of your IPP doesn't just indulge in the rest stops... It enjoys the ride. It lives in the knowledge that bliss is not just at the stop, but on the road. And make no mistake, how you travel the road, is how you will roam the shops at the stop. Who you are, and how you live on the journey, is the you that you will have with you to enjoy the prophecy's manifestation once you arrive at what you say you've always wanted. So, be the best "you" now. If you can't enjoy the ride, you won't enjoy the arrival. Joy is not destination-specific. It is a way of being - a practice that you choose to apply, all day and all night.

You can choose to live in the joy and light of a "you" that has everything you've ever wanted, operates from a place of peace, is guided by a prophetic projection and is delighted with every divine being and experience encountered along the way. You can tap the spirit inside of you that knows all there is to know, has all that's truly real and playfully enjoys the abundance of this illusion of reality on which we journey. You simply have to make the conscious effort to consistently choose to embody the highest version of who you are. So, are you ready to do that? Can you begin today, right now?... Damn right you can!

Poetic Reflection: Work, Process, Modify

Work, process, modify
Work, process, modify
It may sound too clinical,
Sound like it's too difficult
Feel like in the big scheme of everything you need, it's simply
just not worth your time
To try and learn these random skills, all in an attempt to be
the type of person who has complete control over their mind
I mean, that's not even possible anyway, right?
Plus, right now you're just trying to survive
Stay alive
Keep on your grind
And keep your eyes on some other prize
Anyway, everyone knows that this therapeutic, self-help, new
age stuff is nothing but a lie
And you've been doing things your way for a long time so...
So, you figure, you'll be fine
But trust me when I tell you that arrogance is not kind
And you deserve all the best of the best
That right now, you can't seem to get
So, this right here, is a necessary mountain for you to learn
how to climb,
I mean let's be honest
The truth is that you've been banging your head into the same
wall for a long damn time
And crying about the pain
But you can't seem to figure out why things always end up the
same
Why there's so much pain
Why the negative emotions keep you tied up in chains
And why you can't seem to rid yourself of the stuff about
which you've come to constantly complain

Because, sweetheart... you can't get a different result from
doing the same stuff that you always do,
If you're really trying to get a different result, you're gonna
have to try something new. So...
Work, process, modify
Work, process, modify
Work those thoughts until you have a profound sense of their
impact
Work to keep the helpful, most faith-filled ones in tact
Work to focus on those that bring out the greatest version of
you
And replace the stuff you were taught to think about why you
should be afraid
With the memories of the many ways
That the universe has come through for you
Work your thoughts
Process your feelings
Sit inside every breath of anguish in every uncomfortable
emotion that you may feel
Figure out what's the trigger, what's the trauma, what's your
ego and what's real
And make choices to respond in ways that honor the you that
you're trying to create
The you that came into this world, knowing your fate
A fate bound by no limitations of time and space
It's never too late
Make the choice to heal by learning to process how you feel
That way you can modify your behavior
I'm not asking you to change the spunk that God gave ya
Or the pieces of what you do that help the true essence of
your soul shine through
I'm just asking you to make different choices when you wake
up tomorrow

Choices that will begin to maximize your joy and minimize
your sorrow
Choices that will change the story you tell about who you are
and why you do what you do
Choices that will reveal and represent the greatest version of
you
Because we can all grow in ways that will enrich our lives,
But if you want that growth to be sustainable, you gotta
Work, process and modify

Conclusion

The three and a half decades that preceded this manuscript brought with them innumerable ups and downs, highs and lows. Love and loneliness coexisted, like a braid with two intertwining cords, choking me in the middle. Sure, there were men, but because I had not yet fallen in love with myself, truly falling in love with them was difficult. The infatuations were intense. The connections were genuine. So many times, they seemed promising. But then again, it's easy to get swept off your feet when you're not very grounded. As I learned, the journey of getting to know yourself and growing is the first step toward engaging in true healthy love. Step two is getting to know someone else and both of you committing to mutual, continuous growth, both together and apart.

I didn't have a clue. It's so easy to miss a lot about a person, when our need to have him/her fulfil our "happily ever after", overpowers our desire to truly get to know the person we're casting in that role. You overlook stuff... About them and about yourself. That's why, even with men to fill my heart and romance to fill my days, it was loneliness who became the guardian of my evenings. It was the only thing that comforted me in the face of infidelity and somehow also soothed and amplified my pain. That's why we spent years hanging out with nights of lying awake.

The ten years of my twenties were the best of times for loneliness and me. Our friendship, turned romance, soon became the one dependable presence upon which I could rely. And though other love interests came and went, my affair with loneliness remained a constant. We would break up to make up, lose sight of our union, separate and entertain other interests. But something always pulled us back together.

First there was Mr. Marmalade Skin and his "walks" that led to women. I dedicated so much time and energy to being with him that I chose to be unfaithful to myself in the process. That is, until loneliness returned to take his place. Then it was all about us for a while. But soon I was caught up in Caramel Eyes. It was a romance for which I made so many moral sacrifices and compromises that I just couldn't bring myself to cut the losses and walk away... until the damage was so great, the romance was so bitter, and the love hurt so deep. By that time, loneliness and I had long rekindled our affair and its heat seemed to just melt the caramel away. So, we tried to make it work again, loneliness and me. But before you knew it, I was back in love and breaking up with loneliness. Then my marriage to Mr. Cinnamon Smile turned to an incubator for loneliness and its friends and back together we were; me and loneliness once more.

The period of solitude that followed my marital separation was one of the saddest chapters of my tale. The hurt and disappointment were just too strong. The tears just wouldn't stop. I could feel a prolonged agony linger in my abdomen throughout the most basic of daily functions. Getting out of bed was excruciating. Getting into bed was frightening. Anything that left me alone with my thoughts felt hellish. Anything that forced me to interact with others felt pressured. I struggled with even the easiest of tasks: showering, cleaning, eating. Life felt impossible to push through. My relationship with loneliness no longer felt like a pain that I could tolerate.

Now that we could finally be together, the intensity was just more than I could bear. With no third party for our threesome, there was no buffer for the pain. It now just felt burdensome, stressful, sad. My faithless thoughts, painful feelings and toxic behaviors were eating away at any little bit of peace that had survived the storm. I was trapped in patterns that I didn't even see as harmful and yet all of life was becoming too much. I kept thinking that it would never get better - that this painful sting would never cease - that maybe I didn't deserve to be happy because of my "sins" with Caramel. I thought this was my one chance and it was now over. I was sure I would not recover.

What limits we place on ourselves, on one another, on God and the entire universe, when we choose to believe these stories in our head. How scary the world becomes, how scary we can become, if we choose to believe that we are anything other than fabulous! But the good news is it doesn't have to be that way. There's a part of you noticing those parts of you that need help. In there, under all that, is a you unscathed by the brainwashing; aware and enlightened. And its voice becoming louder in your head right now, is enough to show you that you aren't destined to live in this confusion. Your true nature - your spirit - is ready to take over the wheel as you proceed on this journey. That's what happened for me.

I began to realize, as the desperation and anxiety sunk in, that I could never be happy in this "on again-off again" affair with loneliness to which the most masochistic parts of my ego had now become addicted. This tormented love story had become abusive. I had to find a way to come to terms with solitude so that I would no longer be afraid of loneliness or be swept away by it. I needed to be free of this feeling. I needed to make peace with being alone.

The years that followed that epiphany marked a time of transformation for my soul. I considered the "whys" of choices that I made and challenged the motivations that I found. I survived days and nights of what I thought would be endless cries and used my survival to rebuild my confidence that I could survive. I learned to sit still in thought and worked to control those thoughts until the pain of my beliefs would fade into faith. I re-developed my faith, accepted myself as part of a larger energetic force and moved toward a sense of connectedness with all beings. I said good-bye to alcohol. I welcomed the world of boundaries. I re-examined my communication styles and went the extra mile to learn to be more effective. I took vows of celibacy and spent years outside of relationships.

Every day I learned a little more about myself until I could embrace my strengths and my limitations from a true place of humility. Then I learned some more. I completed my doctorate, was promoted four times and moved into six-figure salaries doing work that helped others live better. I danced and crocheted and worked on every issue that I saw get in the way of my joy. From the thoughts in my head to the words that came out of my mouth, I took control of my consciousness. I traveled the world visiting churches in Spain, mosques in Istanbul and temples throughout Thailand, curiously absorbing what the masters know – the value of silence, the usefulness of faith, the ease of joy. I walked the beaches of a half-dozen tropical islands and met God in the waves. I learned to practice gratitude every day. I meditated atop the Great Wall of China and rode camels in Morocco. I made a vow to truly live: to make every day count, to act on my vision, be of service, realize my purpose, and smile in heart.

And in that space of very hard work and pain turned joyous, I learned to love being alone. Once I was ready, willing and capable of staring loneliness in its eyes, it seemed to just vanish. And the better I got at acknowledging the blessings around me and within me, the more I loved myself, and the more I enjoyed spending time with myself until time alone made me feel free. And then I began to search for that feeling in all my experiences and got rid of what did not fit. And soon, in my moments of being alone, my best friend was me. We had a good run, loneliness and me. But there was no longer a place for our love in this new world of self-love that I had created. Being alone no longer felt lonely and being in pain no longer felt permanent. My soul had power. My thoughts were fleeting. My joy was constant and in solitude, I found peace.

It's been quite the journey. I worked my thoughts, processed my feelings and modified my behavior in each of the eight dimensions of wellness. I read more, wrote more and went back to sketching which rejuvenated my intellect. I focused on being more emotionally healthy by meditating more, actively working to change internally and engaging only in romantic relationships that encourage the greatest version of me. I became more spiritually aligned by embracing humility, gratitude and patience. I reached new occupational heights by believing in my dreams, doing what I love to do and learning how to love life even in the moments that seem tough. Financially, I've seen a major pay-off by learning to believe in abundance and continuing to invest in myself. For instance, saving money that I then reallocated toward my wellness work. I learned to be more honest, more selective and more vulnerable, which completely transformed my social life. I learned to honor my body by giving it adequate rest, watching what I put in it and keeping it active. Most interestingly, I gained a true appreciation for nature, the value of a tranquil and inspirationally-decorated space and the importance of living how and where you feel the freest. And while I still have so much to learn and so far to go, I couldn't be more elated with how far I've come, and I want the same for you.

Today I woke up excited about my life. This is now a feeling that I can't shake, nor do I want to. It follows me around my day. It lies with me at night and whispers thoughts into my mind that make me smile and help me to relax. It's the feeling that I am exactly who I want to be AND that I am exactly where I'm supposed to be. Today I woke up excited to be me. I've been feeling this way a lot lately. Again, being alone no longer feels lonely. On the contrary, I never felt better accompanied. I rarely feel more serene than when I am left to my thoughts, feelings and faith. And while I'm still doing the hard work of healing, I no longer dread what's in my mind. That's mostly because I now think much more about joy than I do about pain, and I make choices guided by light. I make choices that feel strong to my soul and help me feel at peace when I am sleeping and energized when I'm up.

As far as my romantic relationships go, I feel comfortable saying that under the scars of my past is the heart of a hopeless romantic who has once again fallen in love. This time, first with myself, and then with a man who has one of the kindest spirits; whose touch is enchanting and whose love feels pure – *Mr. Perfect For Me.* He's doing the same kind of hard work - learning from his wounds - and together we have commenced a journey more spiritual than those of the other romances upon which either of us has previously embarked. He too just recently fell in love with himself, and because we have each professed ourselves eternal students and teachers, we are now in a place where our partnership feels as Godly as love can. Day in and day out, we practice being together, being alone, being at peace, being in love, being patient, being clear, being curious, being grateful and being supportive of one another. We laugh, we kiss, we dream, and we think in a way that honors our connection to each other, to God and to ourselves, in no particular order. And though we fall short of practicing alignment with our highest truth on many occasions, those are the days when we work the hardest to listen, speak, meditate, pray and grow to be healthier together.

We hope this union takes us into the reaches of time. But we feel equally honored by the uncertainty that surrounds every relationship. We know that we are safe in the hands of the universe, that we are strong enough to progress from all pain and that with any number of possible paths comes a whole new set of beginnings, joys, wounds and lessons through which we strengthen our relationship with ourselves and with God.

I got some pressure to write more about my romance with *Mr. Perfect For Me*, from many of the people who read rough drafts of this work. After all, he's such a big part of my life and our love is so delicious, how could I not say more? It was tempting, and perhaps I will in the next book. But not here. He and I both felt strongly in favor of this book's message: the relationship with self is the pay-off. The happy, healthy and exciting romantic relationship that he and I are building, is just one of the many blessings that you attract when you get right with yourself.

That's what I want you to take from all this. When you put this book down, feel the shift taking place in your spirit and let it remind you of the greatness that you have inside. Let all your fears of loneliness give way to an eagerness to get to know yourself better and when you feel the craving for love, remember to first and foremost...

LOVE

YOU

Poetic Reflection: My Prayer for You

I pray you enjoyed the book you've just read,
I pray that at night, in the midst of twilight, when you've laid
your body down to rest in your bed
When you begin to replay
The trials and triumphs of your entire day
In images that pop in and out of your head
I pray that you take heed to the words that I've said
Or better yet, that you find inspiration in the lessons that I've
shared here
I pray that you can grow like the seed of joy planted in every
tear
I pray that you find the courage to challenge everything that
you now fear
I pray that you cherish every second of every minute of every
hour of every day that you're here
I hope that you can hold each of those seconds dear
I hope it's become clear
That your happiness and your wellness are intimately
connected
And that every second spent on developing yourself is time
well invested
Because self-care and serenity will always be tied together
And it's not selfish of you to focus on making yourself, your
relationships and your world better
I pray you're pleased to find that life is kind and will return to
you whatever energy you give it
I pray that you fight to transform the trauma of your past into
a transcendental triumph of spirit
I pray you modify your behavior, change your thoughts and
process your feelings
I pray that in this work, you find the healing you've been
seeking

I pray you nurture your emotions, finances, spirit, social life, occupation, intellect, environment and physical body
I pray that you align with your intuitive, pre-cognitive prophecy
And I welcome you to the bliss that comes with falling in love with yourself, moving from loneliness to wellness and enjoying how you'll be living
For this may seem like the end, but my love, it is truly only the beginning!

And for my Latinas in particular,
I pray that the novelas in your life grow to be less dramatic,
And that you allow yourself, always, to be the protagonist,
That not just your endings are happy but your story as well
and that you don't just succeed but that you propel.
I pray that you find fulfillment as a happy jamona or as an enlightened esposa, lo que sea tu cosa!
Because the truth is that there's no right or wrong way to set yourself free
Just love you first, foremost and unapologetically
Each and every day and in perpetuity,
Remember that de dicho a hecho hay un buen trecho,
And change requires that you challenge yourself steadfastly,
But also enjoy life and all the blessings it gave ya,
And leave in your mark on the world, some of that Latina flava.

REFERENCED & RECOMMENDED

Bain & Company, Inc. (2012). A World Awash in Money Capital Trends Through 2020 (pp. 1-29, Report). Bain & Company, Inc. Retrieved December 19, 2016, from http://www.bain.com/Images/BAIN_REPORT_A_worl d_awash_in_money.pdf

Beck, Judith S. (2011). Cognitive Behavior Therapy, Second Edition: Basics and Beyond. New York: Guilford Publications, Inc.

Beck, Martha. (2001). Finding your own North Star: claiming the life you were meant to live. New York: Crown.

Boehm, J. K., & Lyubomirsky, S. (2008). Does Happiness Promote Career Success? Journal Of Career Assessment, 1-16. Retrieved December 19, 2016, from http://citeseerx.ist.psu.edu/viewdoc/summary?doi=10.1.1.378.6546

Brinke, L. T., Lee, J. J., & Carney, D. R. (2015). The physiology of (dis)honesty: does it impact health? ScienceDirect: Current Opinion in Psychology,6, 177-182. Retrieved December 20, 2016, from http://www.leannetenbrinke.com/uploads/2/1/0/4/210 49652/ten_brinke_lee_carney_2015.pdf

Bronfenbrenner, U., Vasta, Ross (Ed), (1992). Six theories of child development: Revised formulations and current issues. (pp. 187-249). London, England: Jessica Kingsley Publishers, p.285.

Cacioppo, John T.; Hughes, Mary Elizabeth; Waite, Linda J.; Hawkley, Louise C. and Thisted, Ronald A. (2006). "Loneliness as a specific risk factor for depressive symptoms: Cross-sectional and longitudinal analyses." Psychology and Aging, Vol 21(1), March p.140-151.

Chandler, C. K., Holden, J. M., & Kolander, C. A. (1992). "Counseling for spiritual wellness: Theory and practice." Journal of Counseling & Development, 71(2), 168-175.

Cofresí, N. I. (1999). Gender Roles in Transition among Professional Puerto Rican Women. Frontiers: A Journal of Women Studies,20(1), 161. doi:10.2307/3346999

Cooley, Charles H. (1902). Human Nature and the Social Order. New York: Scribner's, 1902. Confer pp. 183–184

Davis , D. M., & Hayes, J. A. (2011). What Are the Benefits of Mindfulness? A Practice Review of Psychotherapy-Related Research. Psychotherapy,48(2), 198-208. Retrieved December 19, 2016, from http://www.apa.org/pubs/journals/features/pst-48-2-198.pdf

De Francisco Vela, S., Casais, M., & Desmet, P. (2014). Feeding Your Piggy Bank with Intentions: A study on saving behaviour, saving strategies, and happiness. Social Innovation, 64-69. Retrieved December 20, 2016, from http://studiolab.ide.tudelft.nl/diopd/wp-content/uploads/2015/11/DeFrancisco-FeedingYourPiggyBank2014.pdf

Desmet, P. M. (2015). Design for Mood: Twenty Activity-Based Opportunities to Design for Mood Regulation. International Journal of Design,9(2), 1-19. Retrieved December 20, 2016, from http://www.ijdesign.org/ojs/index.php/IJDesign/article/viewFile/2167/685

Duffy, R. D., & Dik, B. J. (2013). Research on calling: What have we learned and where are we going? Journal of Vocational Behavior,83, 428-436. Retrieved December 19, 2016, from

http://www.drryanduffy.com/uploads/3/1/7/2/317244
47/duffy__dik_2013.pdf

Dyer, W. W. (2004). The power of intention: learning to co-
create your world your way. Carlsbad, CA: Hay House.

Emmons, R. A., & Stern, R. (2013). Gratitude as a
Psychotherapeutic Intervention. Journal of Clinical
Psychology: In Session,69(8), 846-855. Retrieved
December 19, 2016, from http://ei.yale.edu/wp-
content/uploads/2013/11/jclp22020.pdf

Flynn, F. J., & Bohns, V. K. (2008). If You Need Help, Just
Ask: Underestimating Compliance with Direct Requests
for Help. Cornell University, ILR School, ILR
Collection, 1-30. Retrieved December 20, 2016, from
http://digitalcommons.ilr.cornell.edu/cgi/viewcontent.cg
i?article=2092&context=articles

Fortin, A. H., Dwamena, F. C., Frankel, R. M., & Smith, R.C.
(2012). Smith's Patient-Centered Interviewing: An
Evidence-Based Method, Third Edition. New York:
McGraw Hill Professional.

Foundation for Inner Peace. (1985). A Course in Miracles.
Tiburon, CA: Foundation for Inner Peace.

Gardner, M., & Steinberg, L. (2005). Peer Influence on Risk
Taking, Risk Preference, and Risky Decision Making in
Adolescence and Adulthood: An Experimental
Study. Developmental Psychology,41(4), 625-635.
Retrieved from
https://secure.uwf.edu/smathews/documents/peerrolein
risktakinggardnerandsteinberg.pdf.

Gilbert, Elizabeth. (2007). Eat, Pray, Love: One Woman's
Search for Everything Across Italy, India and Indonesia.
New York: Penguin Group, Inc.

----------------------. (2011). Committed: A Love Story. New York: Penguin Group, Inc.

Goleman, D. (1995). Emotional intelligence. New York: Bantam Books.

Gross, J. J. (2007). Handbook of emotion regulation. New York: Guilford Press.

Hawkins, M. (2009). Activating your ambition: A guide to coaching the best out of yourself and others. Dallas, TX.: Brown Books Pub.

Hay, L. L. (2004). You can heal your life. Carlsbad, CA: Hay House.

Hicks, E., & Hicks, J. (2004). Ask and it is given: Learning to manifest your desires. Carlsbad, CA: Hay House.

Human Kinetics. (2010). Health and wellness for life. Champaign, IL: Human Kinetics.

Ilibagiza, I., & Erwin, S. (2006). Left to tell: discovering God amidst the Rwandan holocaust. Carlsbad, CA: Hay House, Inc.

Keniger, L. E., Gaston, K. J., Irvine, K. N., & Fuller, R. A. (2013). What are the Benefits of Interacting with Nature? International Journal of Environmental Research and Public Health,10, 913-935. Retrieved December 20, 2016, from https://espace.library.uq.edu.au/view/UQ:298590/UQ29 8590.pdf.

Khaw, K., Wareham, N., Bingham, S., Welch, A., Luben, R., & Day, N. (2008). Combined Impact of Health Behaviours and Mortality in Men and Women: The

EPIC-Norfolk Prospective Population Study. PLoS Medicine,5(1), 39-47. Retrieved December 20, 2016, from http://journals.plos.org/plosmedicine/article/file?id=10. 1371/journal.pmed.0050012&type=printable

Kupersmidt, J. B., Sigda, K. B., Voegler, M. E. & Sedikides, C. (1999). Social self-discrepancy theory and loneliness during childhood and adolescence (pp. 263-279). In K. Rotenberg & S. Hymel (Eds.) Loneliness in childhood and adolescence. New York: Cambridge University Press.

Masi CM, Chen HY, Hawkley LC, Cacioppo JT. (2010). "A meta-analysis of interventions to reduce loneliness." Personality and Social Psychology Review.15(3):219-66. Aug 17

Matz, S. C., Gladstone, J. J., & Stillwell, D. (2016). Money Buys Happiness When Spending Fits Our Personality. Psychological Science, 1-11. Retrieved from http://foxfellowship.yale.edu/sites/default/files/files/M oney%20Buys%20Happiness%20When%20Spending%20 Fits%20Our%20Personality%20(1).pdf

Miller-Perrin, C. L., & Mancuso, E. K. (2015). Faith from a positive psychology perspective. Dordrecht: Springer.

Millman, Daniel. (1980). Way of the Peaceful Warrior: A Book That Changes Lives. Tiburon, CA: H.J. Kramer, Inc.

--------------------. (2004). The Sacred Journey of the Peaceful Warrior. Tiburon, CA: H.J. Kramer, Inc.

--------------------. (2006). The Journey of Socretes: An Adventure. New York: Harper Collins, Inc.

Morin, A. (2011). Self-Awareness Part 1: Definition, Measures, Effects, Functions, and Antecedents. Social and Personality Psychology Compass, 807-823. Retrieved

December 19, 2016, from
http://citeseerx.ist.psu.edu/viewdoc/download?doi=10.1
.1.405.362&rep=rep1&type=pdf

Nickerson, R. S. (1998). Confirmation bias: A ubiquitous
phenomenon in many guises. Review of General
Psychology, 2(2), 175-220. doi:10.1037/1089-2680.2.2.175

Olson, D. H., Olson, A. K., & Larson, P. J. (2012).
PREPARE-ENRICH Program: Overview and New
Discoveries about Couples. Journal of Family &
Community Ministries,25, 30-44. Retrieved December 19,
2016, from https://www.prepare-
enrich.com/pe/pdf/research/newdiscoveries.pdf

Pehrsson, D. E., & McMillen, P. (2007). Bibliotherapy:
Overview and implications for counselors (ACAPCD-02).
Alexandria, VA: American Counseling Association.
Retrieved December 18, 2016, from
https://www.counseling.org/resources/library/ACA%20
Digests/ACAPCD-02.pdf

Peplau, L. A., and Perlman, D. (1981). "Toward a Social
Psychology of Loneliness in Personal Relationships in
Disorders" edited by S. Duck and R. Gilmour. London:
Academic Press.

Peplau, L. A., and Perlman, D., eds. (1982). Loneliness: A
Sourcebook of Current Theory, Research, and Therapy.
New York: Wiley.

Pichot, T., & Dolan, Y. (2003). Solution-focused brief therapy:
Its effective use in agency settings. Binghamton, NY:
Haworth.

Robert Wood Johnson Foundation Commission to Build a
Healthier America. (2008). Where We Live Matters for
Our Health: Neighborhoods and Health (pp. 1-11,

Report). Robert Wood Johnson Foundation Commission to Build a Healthier America. Retrieved December 19, 2016, from http://www.commissiononhealth.org/PDF/888f4a18-eb90-45be-a2f8-159e84a55a4c/Issue%20Brief%203%20Sept%2008%20-%20Neighborhoods%20and%20Health.pdf

Rottinghaus, P. J., Hees, C. K., & Conrath, J. A. (2009). Enhancing job satisfaction perspectives: Combining Holland themes and basic interests. Journal of Vocational Behavior,75, 139-151. Retrieved December 19, 2016, from http://www.choixdecarriere.com/pdf/5873/Rottinghaus HeesConrath-2009.pdf

Rowatt, W. C., Powers, C., Targhetta, V., Comer, J., Kennedy, S., & Labouff, J. (2006). Development and initial validation of an implicit measure of humility relative to arrogance. The Journal of Positive Psychology,1(4), 198-211. Retrieved December 19, 2016, from http://www.baylor.edu/content/services/document.php /35616.pdf

Sandberg, S. (2013). Lean in: women, work, and the will to lead. New York: Alfred A. Knopf.

Santiago, Esmeralda. (1993). When I was Puerto Rican. Reading, MA: Addison-Wesley,

Shakur, A., Davis, A. Y., & Hinds, L. S. (2001). Assata: an autobiography. Chicago, IL: L. Hill Books.

Shumaker, S. A., Ockene, J. K., & Riekert, K. A. (Eds.). (2008). The Handbook of Health Behavior Change, Third Edition. New York, NY: Springer Publishing Company.

Slayton, S. C., D'Archer, J., & Kaplan, F. (2010). Outcome Studies on the Efficacy of Art Therapy: A Review of Findings. Art Therapy: Journal of the American Art Therapy Association, 27(3), 108-118. Retrieved December 19, 2016, from http://arttherapy.org/upload/outcomes.pdf

Sotomayor, S. (2013). My beloved world. New York: Knopf.

Spielmann, Stephanie S., MacDonald, Geoff; Maxwell, Jessica A.; Joel, Samantha; Peragine, Diana; Muise, Amy; Impett, Emily A. (2013). "Settling for Less Out of Fear of Being Single." Journal of Personality and Social Psychology. Vol 105(6), Dec:1049-1073.

Steiner, C. (2003). Emotional literacy: Intelligence with a heart. Fawnskin, CA: Personhood Press.

Stuckey, H. L., & Nobel, J. (2010). The Connection Between Art, Healing, and Public Health: A Review of Current Literature. Retrieved December 18, 2016, from https://www.ncbi.nlm.nih.gov/pmc/articles/PMC28046 29/

Swarbrick, M. (2006). A Wellness Approach. Psychiatric Rehabilitation Journal, 29 (4) 311- 3314.

Szabo, A. (2003). Acute Psychological Benefits of Exercise Performed at Self-Selected Workloads: Implications for Theory and Practice. Journal of Sports Science and Medicine,2, 77-87. Retrieved December 20, 2016, from http://www.jssm.org/vol2/n3/2/v2n3-2pdf.pdf

Tolle, E. (2006). A new earth: Awakening to your life's purpose. New York: Plume.

Vingerhoets, A. J., Nyklíček, I., & Denollet, J. (2008). Emotion regulation: Conceptual and clinical issues. New York, NY: Springer.

Walker, M. P. (2009). The Role of Sleep in Cognition and Emotion. The Year In Cognitive Neuroscience, 168-197. Retrieved December 20, 2016, from https://walkerlab.berkeley.edu/reprints/Walker_NYAS_2009.pdf.

Walsch, Neale Donald. (1996). Conversations with God: An Uncommon Dialogue Book I. New York: G.P. Putnam's Sons.

--------------------------. (1998). Conversations with God: An Uncommon Dialogue Book II. Charlottesville, VA: Hampton Roads Publishing Company, Inc.

--------------------------. (1998). Conversations with God: An Uncommon Dialogue Book III. Charlottesville, VA: Hampton Roads Publishing Company, Inc.

Weiss, Robert S. (1973). Loneliness: The experience of emotional and social isolation. Cambridge, MA, US: The MIT

Williamson, Marianne. (1992). A return to love: reflections on the principles of a course in miracles. New York, NY: HarperCollins.

Yousafzai, M., & Lamb, C. (2015). I am Malala: the girl who stood up for education and was shot by the Taliban. New York: Back Bay Books, Little Brown and Company.

Made in the USA
San Bernardino, CA
18 August 2018